Alex

Thanks for...

Coloring
Outside
the Lines™

2ND EDITION!

Coloring Outside the Lines™

2ND EDITION!

Business Thoughts on Creativity, Marketing and Sales

From the crayon of
Jeff Tobe

Original drawings by Jordan Tobe, age 9

The Business Conference Press
Monroeville, Pennsylvania

First printing 2001
Second printing 2001
Third printing 2002
SECOND EDITION printing 2004

ISBN 0-9662689-2-X

LCCN 00-133195

ATTENTION CORPORATIONS, UNIVERSITIES, COLLEGES AND PROFESSIONAL ORGANIZATIONS: Quantity discounts are available on bulk purchases of this book and the book can be completely customized for your organization to fit specific needs. Contact us at 1-800-875-7106 or at Coloring Outside the Lines, 200 James Place Suite 400 Monroeville PA 15146.

To the primary colorers in my life...
Judy, Maya and Jordan

Thanks for always putting up with my coloring!

And to my Dad...I never did get you that white Cadillac,
but I got to mention you in my book!

THOUGHTS ON...CREATIVITY

THOUGHTS ON...MARKETING

THOUGHTS ON...SALES

THOUGHTS ON...

Creativity

If you Can't Win the Game...

On Competition and Changing the Way You Look at Business

Recently, I sat down to play a Chutes-and-Ladders-type game with my eight-year-old daughter. It was a lot of fun to see her little mind at work, but she had one annoying peculiarity: she was continually bending the rules, reshaping roles, changing the boundaries and reversing strategies. Everything I took for granted, she challenged. Cheating? I don't think so.

When we decide that we are in competition, we implicitly agree to play the game the way it has always been played, to abide by the formal and informal rules and roles, as well as the unspoken rituals. Although competing can be fun and exciting, it is not very creative and definitely limits the imagination. It is because of this experience that I have concluded that *competition encourages conformity.*

Kids are always changing the rules and the way the game is played. Research shows that kids spend more time creating and re-creating a game than actually playing it. So, why not ignore the competition and start to re-create the way the "Business Game" is played??

When you compete head-on, you are just agreeing to play by the old rules...to conform to the way it has always been done...to stay in the lines! Innovation simply means to change the way we do things. I believe that there is no such thing as a new idea-only new was of presenting old ones. This hits at the very core of our business persona. Once you make the decision not to "compete", but to define your own market, you can find solace in the fact that you don't have to "re-invent the wheel" to be successful. Approach the market with the mindset that you are simply going to find new ways to present what you already have. Maybe that means simply presenting your service, your product or yourself differently.

When you begin to accept competition as a head-to-head battle, then there are no winners and you tend to lose any advantage you ever had in your marketplace. Look at what has happened with airline frequent-flier programs. What was once a very unique, innovative idea now has been copied so many times that no airline has the advantage in this arena. As a matter of fact, I would venture to guess that there is many an airline executive who rues the day that the concept of frequent flier bonuses was ever developed.

It would be naive and foolish of me to say "Don't compete". I realize that anything you can do nowadays to beat your competition to the punch can give you some small advantage in the marketplace. Though you will gain one-time "one ups" on your competitors by facing them head-on, competing will never present the break-throughs that you are going to need to really move ahead of the pack nor the staying power you need to survive in your business.

Remember, every new and innovative idea in any business has always—ALWAYS—broken with tradition. I love to repeat the advertising copy of one of the large auto-makers, *"THIS IS NOT YOUR FATHER'S OLDSMOBILE".*

This is not the way your business has been

conducted in the past. I have enjoyed challenging many audiences to *"stop looking in their windshields to see how it has always been done in the past. Start looking through your windshield to see what is coming down the road ahead of you in your profession."* If you spend your time considering the way things have always been done in your organization, you are not prioritizing your energies.

Start asking yourself, "How can I present my company's 'experience' differently than all the others professing to be in the same business?"

By changing the rules to the game, you get outside of your comfort zone and begin looking at volatile business challenges from a whole new perspective. We are not going to be comfortable any longer and we can either accept the challenge or get left behind. Wayne Gretzky, one of the all-time greatest hockey players of our time, was once asked by a reporter how it was that he always managed to be where the puck is. With much thought, Gretzky replied, "I'm not always where the puck is. I am always where the puck is going to be!" Are you where your profession is, or are you where your profession is going to be?

Helen Keller once said, "The most pathetic person in world is someone who has sight but has no vision". Rather than looking at the competition that *is*, why not start to create what *ISN'T*?

Lessons From the Pump

Do People Go Out of Their Way to Do Business With You?

On a business trip to Washington, DC, I experienced one of those days where everything went wrong from beginning to end. Not only were the day's business dealings a complete flop, but the 250 mile drive back to Pittsburgh, PA looked like it was going to be a disaster as well. As I approached the halfway point—an exchange on the Pennsylvania turnpike called "Breezewood"—I glanced at my gas gage and realized that it read empty. I decided to treat myself and I pulled into a full-serve bay; a luxury of which I rarely partake!

Before I could even get my car into park, a young man of about fourteen years threw open the service station door and ran to my car in the pouring rain. I repeat—HE RAN TO MY CAR! From under the brim of his oil stained and rain soaked ball cap, his eyes gleamed and he smiled as he greeted me.

"Hiya sir! Can I help you?"

I was in no mood to be friendly. "Just fill it up," I said rather flatly.

As he approached the rear of my car, he began to whistle loudly. Now, understand that it was freezing outside, this kid is getting soaked and he is whistling. I looked in my rear view mirror and panicked as I watched as he proceeded to jam my gas cap into the nozzle to make the gas empty into my car on its own accord. Why the horror? I realized that this left him free to come back up to talk to me. I didn't want to talk to this kid—he was a little too friendly for me.

"So, havin' a bad day are ya?" he deduced. "What do ya do for a livin'?" I wasn't going to get into training and consulting with a fourteen-year-old, so I proclaimed myself a motivational speaker.

He smiled a knowing smile and proclaimed, "SO AM I!"

NOW HE HAD MY ATTENTION. I immediately asked, "How are you a motivational speaker?" He looked me straight in the eye and explained, "Well, I'm not really a speaker, but I am motivational!" He continued, "Isn't your job to get in front of people and get them up and going?" I nodded in agreement. "My job is to stick the nozzle in and keep them going!"

I would agree that his answer was a little bizarre. This young kid had taught me two very valuable lessons in life. The first is simply to look at what you do from a different perspective. The second, and most important, is that people want to do business with people who seem to enjoy what they do for a living. This kid obviously enjoyed what he did for a living and for the past few years I stop at that gas station in hopes of getting that kid to pump my gas. And the sad thing is that he doesn't even work there anymore. He's in college. I'm just hoping he will graduate and come back to pump gas!

Do people go out of their way to do business with you? Is the experience such a memorable one that they will keep coming back?

The Rock

As Long as Your Goal Doesn't Change
and They Use the Tools You Give Them —
Who Cares How They Get There?

In another lifetime—and I don't mean a "Shirley MacLaine" other lifetime—I was a manufacturer's representative. One year, the powers-that-be of the company I represented decided to get creative. Instead of bringing all of the territory managers to the factory to see the new line of goods, they decided to subject us all to an Outward Bound experience.

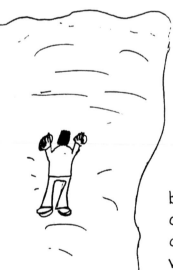

For those of you unfamiliar with this, Outward Bound has numerous locations and offers a leadership/team building experience based around a certain activity depending on where in the world it is located. The Outward Bound program

10

in which we participated, was based in Leadville, Colorado, and was centered around rock climbing.

Please understand that, in my lifetime, I never had any ambition to climb a ladder for fun, never mind a large rock! But it was one of those things where the company said "be there" and you had better show. For the first five and one-half hours on the first day, they took us out and positioned the first four of us at the base of a sheer ninety-foot rock face and proclaimed, "You are going to climb to the top."

This may not sound like a lot of rock to some of you, but just imagine nine stories of jagged rock rising straight above you. I needed more of an incentive than some guy just telling me to climb the rock...so I made one up!

I turned to Craig on my left and challenged him. "I'll bet you twenty-five dollars I can get to the top first," I proclaimed. Craig didn't hesitate. "You're on," he said confidently. I hadn't even considered my other two colleagues on my other side, but they chimed in that they were in the race as well. Now it was nine stories of rock worth a hundred dollars! I had my incentive.

Each one of us had a separate guide from Outward Bound. I will never forget Joe, my rock climbing mentor, because, at that point Joe whispered in my ear; "For fifty bucks, I'll get you there first!" I guessed that this was the teambuilding that they referred to in the brochures! I shook on it.

Joe took me aside and explained in a whispered tone, "Don't let the others hear. Do you see that rock sticking out at about two and a half feet?" I nodded. "When you start, stick your right foot on that ledge and boost yourself up. Next, see that rock, right here at eye level? Grab that rock with your right hand and pull yourself up. The secret to winning, Jeff, is that branch without any leaves on it, at about twelve feet. Grab that branch with your left hand and pull yourself up. It will hold your weight—I've done this a thousand times before." And, so went the verbal tour up the rest of the rock face.

Someone yelled "Go!" I stepped on the rock with my right foot. I pulled myself up with my right hand. I reached out for that naked twig and couldn't reach it. No matter how hard I tried, I couldn't reach it. At that point, my new partner yelled at me, "Grab the stupid branch". Straining, I replied, "Joe, I can't...I'm going to die!"

Please understand that I was only two and one-half feet off the ground. I had one foot still on the ground. But, I was going to die.

As I was reaching for that branch, I found a rock sticking out at about ten feet that was easier to seize. As I tested it, I found that it would hold my weight, so I pulled myself up. As I did, Joe yelled at me again. "No. No. No. That's not right." Through clenched teeth, I retorted, "It's right for me, Joe".

He yelled at me the entire way up the face of that rock. Did I make it to the top? Absolutely! Did I win? Absolutely not! I am still bitter about that.

What does this experience have to do with creativity-in-business? Everything!

I learned a very valuable lesson while clinging to that rock and being harangued by Joe. As long as I had the knowledge I needed, as long as I used the tools he gave me (ie. the belays, the ropes), and as long as the goal (getting to the top of the rock) didn't change, WHO CARES HOW I GOT THERE?

So many companies with whom I have worked, feel it necessary to micro manage every project. If they would simply educate their team, give them a clear understanding of the goals and present them with the right tools, WHO CARES HOW THEY GOT THERE?

I encourage you to listen to your environment for whispers of opportunity. Your clients, internal and external, are telling you the second right answer to reaching your goals, if you would just listen!

The Opportunity

Reframing Your Professional Problems

I remember calling my office one day while I was traveling. At the time, we had seven or eight account representatives and I recall speaking with all of them on the telephone. After the niceties were out of the way, they all started with the exact same four words: "I have a problem."

"Jeff, I have a problem with an order."

"Jeff, I am having a problem with a client."

"I have a problem with the receptionist."

"I have a problem with the computer."

"I have a problem with the toilet."

I got very sick of the word "problem". Think about it. If you have a problem, you automatically have an obstacle to get over. So, in all of my wisdom, I went to our regular Monday morning meeting the following week and challenged everyone to come up with another word to replace the word "problem."

They did it. They decided on the word "situation". That week when I called in, I heard things like,

"Jeff, I have a *situation* with the receptionist."

"Jeff, I have a *situation* with the toilet."

I felt more like the commander of a naval ship then the owner of my own business. Back to the drawing board.

The following week they came up with a word that has literally changed the way we do business.

The word? *Challenge!*

I know you know the word, but why is it that we won't use it? I have a theory. I think human beings love to have problems. I am not trying to be facetious. I think we rely on it as a great excuse. You see, if the problem is big enough, the obstacle is big enough. And, if the obstacle is big enough, the excuse is justified. I've heard it again and again.

"Sorry boss. Too big an obstacle. I tried but I just couldn't get it done."

Instead, why not change it to the word "challenge"? From every problem comes an obstacle. From every challenge comes an opportunity. So, if we can discover the challenges we face—personally or professionally—we can discover the opportunity it presents to us.

The Harvey Principle

How to See Invisible Opportunities

Peter Drucker, management guru, said "THE ONLY WAY TO PREDICT THE FUTURE IS TO CREATE IT". In these times of turbulent change, you have a unique challenge and a unique opportunity in front of you because you have the capacity to literally create your own future from scratch—literally re-invent it, so to speak. You have to do this with your business or your responsibilities... re-invent what you do. In whatever industry or profession you find yourself, the need to shatter old models of doing business is crucial.

The main principle of creating a more positive, productive and profitable future is something probably fewer than one percent of you—at this

17

point in your career–really understand. I certainly do not mean to be condescending in any way, but I assume that most of you have probably not taken the time to even consider this. This is a principle that, once you understand it, goes far beyond positive thinking, far beyond goal setting, far beyond any of the traditional rules of success. If you understand and apply this principle, you will never be afraid of the future. You will always know that no matter what happens, you can come out of it profitably and productively.

The number one principle in creating a profitable, productive and positive outcome is what I refer to as the HARVEY PRINCIPLE! How many of you remember the imaginary six-foot tall white rabbit, Harvey, from that wonderful 1950 Jimmy Stewart movie of the same name. It suggested that perhaps *the one with the imagination, the innovative one, was not the crazy one after all.*

We have to learn how to see the invisible. To see the invisible opportunities where other people only see visible limitations. To see the invisible potential of the people with whom you work–to see the invisible ideas that change the world. The building in which you work, started as an invisible, intangible idea in the mind of a single person. That person's ability to see the invisible–what was not apparent in physical form–

ultimately produced a structure. Every great invention starts in the mind—in the invisible. Every great entrepreneur sees invisible possibilities—untapped needs—in a marketplace that needs to be served. The most important skill you can learn in creating your own future, is learning the HARVEY PRINCIPLE (like Elwood P. Dowd) seeing what others cannot.

Fortunately, many of your competitors are suffering from what may be an incurable and deadly disease. This disease is a mental disease, not a physical one, and no one has been known to die from it physically...only financially! It's been known to be hazardous to the financial wealth of many individuals and corporations alike. Never fear! I have been able to diagnose this disease. Maybe you can arrest the symptoms—recognize them within yourself or your organization so you won't have to pay thousands to see a specialist after it's too late for you or your company.

It's caused by a virus with the initials B.P.I.D.S.—Business Professionals' Innovation Deficiency Syndrome. BPID Syndrome is a mental infliction that will erode your profits very quickly and keep you office-ridden while your competition is feeling healthy and fit.

The Symptoms

What are the symptoms? I've discovered seven. As I describe them, see if they apply to you, your organization or someone close to you because you could be responsible for curing this dreadful disease and turn out to be a hero. These are the primary reasons that people are unable to see their "Harvey."

#1 Internal Myopia

Are you all familiar with myopia? What is it? *Near-sightedness.* What happens with Internal Myopia is that you are so focused on the internal aspects of your organization—with the business itself—that you can't see the environment. You miss what's happening around you by failing to see the big picture.

#2 Ostrich Syndrome

Ostriches bury their heads in the sand while they leave another part of themselves exposed! If you have the ostrich syndrome, you may not simply ignore reality, you may choose to deny it even exists. There are prob- ably some of you who still deny the fact that informa- tion technology will change the way you do business. There are some people in your industry who deny the fact that their firm can no longer be every-thing to everyone—that you no longer can expect to gain a client for life. I'm not talking about you losing the client as much as I am about the client's infrastructure being likely to change and leave you behind. They have ostrich syndrome.

#3 Past-a-Plegia

What this means is paralysis in the past. This is looking in your rear-view mirror. "What was good enough for the company in the ninety's is good enough nowadays!" I like to coin the words of a large automobile manufacturer when they said, "This is not your father's Oldsmobile," and this is not the way business has been done in the past, yet I find so many organizations suffering from this syndrome. Little things hang around from the past to haunt us.

#4 Psycho-Sclerosis

If you have had any dealings in health care, you may recognize this symptom. It's also known as "My way or the highway." Today, I hear it manifest itself in organizations in the following ways:

"We've never done that before!"

"That's never been done in this profession before!"

"Last time we tried that it didn't work!"

#5 Feedback Immunity

Do you know anyone who is immune to feedback? Sure. This just doesn't mean personal feedback from a superior or peer but, more important, feedback from the marketplace. There are those who choose to ignore this symptom because they are so married to the success of the idea that they are unable to process the feedback of the marketplace when it doesn't work. Because we live in a "customer service oriented environment", I think that this symptom has changed. We MUST respond to our customers' feedback BUT we also have to consider how QUICKLY we respond. It can be something as simple as "How quickly do you return my call when I leave a message on your voice mail?"

#6 Expertitis

This occurs when you know so much about one area nobody can teach you anything new. You've become convinced that all the ideas in that area or field have been invented so you might as well not think any longer. There was a man in the US Patent and Trademark Office who, in 1899 went on a crusade to close the Patent and Trademark

Office. He believed everything that was going to be invented had already been invented! Then he proceeded to ride home on his horse!

#7 Failure-Phobia

This is the fear of making mistakes. In his book *Surviving On Chaos*, Tom Peters talks about how "successful businesses are those who can fail fast and often". Although most people are afraid of making mistakes, you can never learn anything without making them? Most people are not comfortable with the idea of making mistakes-of failing. Mistakes are a necessary byproduct of the whole creative process. *Mistakes are opportunities for learning.*

The Cure

There are 5 steps to curing this syndrome...to seeing your Harvey...to seeing the invisible...to seeing what others are unable to see. These five steps may seem very basic to you at first but as any professional athlete—any Olympian—would quickly remind you, victory often comes from sticking to the basics.

#1 Learn to See the World Through Your Client's Eyes

I would like to relate a story to you that illustrates this better than I could on my own. It's from a book that some of you may be very familiar with—written in the 1950's by G. Lyn Sumner—called *How I Learned the Secrets of Advertising.* He tells a story that perfectly illustrates how important it is to see the world through your client's eyes. As I share this, think about how you can associate this to your business:

"It makes no difference whether you are using a full page ad in a magazine or a five line classified, it is not the space but what you say in that space that determines the success of that advertisement. Let me give you an example: Our maid had left us. and as was the custom in Scranton Pennsylvania, Mrs. Sumner resorted to the method that everyone used to get another one. She called up the *Scranton Times*, an afternoon paper and asked that the following advertisement be inserted in the classified section under HELP WANTED-FEMALE.

"WANTED—Girl for general housework.
727 North Irving Avenue."

The ad ran for 3 days and nothing happened. It was repeated for 3 days more and when still nobody answered it, I made the suggestion that possibly the copy was at fault. Mrs. Sumner said, "All right. You're an advertising writer. If you're so smart, suppose you see what you can do.

I was very professional in my approach. I said it's easy to understand. Here's a solid column of Want Ads all reading the same:

"WANTED–MAID FOR GENERAL HOUSE WORK."

Suppose there is a maid in all of Scranton, who wants a position or wants to change her position, which one of these ads is *she* going to read?

Now, let us put ourselves in the position of the maid herself. Every client has some fault to find with the work we are doing. Every maid has some fault to find with her place of employment. And she has in her mind, her own conception of the ideal place in which to work as every client has in their mind their own perception of their own solution to their own problems.

Let us present our home and all of it's attractiveness in terms of those selling points that will appeal to her. So, I prepared a piece of copy that read like this...

"WANTED...girl to do general housework in small, new home in quiet, attractive hill section. All hardwood floors–easy to keep clean. No washing. No furnace to take care of. Nobody sick. Large, airy maids room. House convenient to 2 bus lines. Small family. Good wages. 727 North Irving Avenue."

Those last two points may have been slightly exaggerated, but after all, they were matters of opinion.

We placed that advertisement in the *Times* on a Thursday when most maids have the afternoon off. The first edition went on the stands at 1 o'clock. By 3, the line of applicants had begun to form on our front porch. By 4 o'clock, buses were erupting maids in groups at our corner. By 5, Mrs. Sumner had made a selection and the appointed one was happily at work in the kitchen a few minutes later getting dinner.

When I came home I got the full story and I proceeded to analyze it. "You see," I explained, "this afternoon dozens of maids, dissatisfied with their jobs read that column of classifieds. And what did they find? They discovered the perfect place to work. The kind of place they'd been thinking and dreaming about."

The trouble was that I didn't let it go at that. Next morning, I went down to the office and told one of the men there what had happened. He looked at me hungrily. "Man, oh man! We've been without a maid for two weeks. I wish you'd write an ad for us". I told him that if he would just give me the specifications of his home as a maid's paradise, I'd be happy to. He gave them to me and, of course, by this time I was getting better at this sort of thing. I wrote an advertisement and he put it in the *Times* the next day.

What do you suppose happened?

Our maid went down and applied for the job!

This story does a great job of illustrating the power of looking at the world through our client's eyes. As basic as this sounds, most of us do not do it! Most of us have no idea of how our customers perceive us, our product or our service. Every morning, take one minute by yourself and imagine you are one of your clients about to do business with you that day. What do they think of when they think of doing business with you?

Do they associate doing business with you as a pain or a pleasure? Are you just another vendor or employee? Are you a valuable, problem-solving resource on whom they can rely? Are you professional? And the key is to do this for each individual client and put yourself in their shoes.

#2 Understand and Embrace Your New Roles in a New World

Almost five hundred years ago, William Shakespeare wrote "All the world's a stage. All the men and women are merely players. They have their exits and their entrances and each in his time plays many parts." Many of us have been playing our 'roles' far too long and in order to create the future, we must re-write our script. I've identified five roles in my one-act play we call the future: one is the lead role and the other four are supporting roles. You must take on these roles in your profession if you are to be more successful. The four supporting roles are as follows:

1. *Challenge solver.* You no longer sell product or services. You solve your clients' challenges. You sell an experience. You look for challenges then find different ways to solve them

2. *Solution broker.* In other words, you provide solutions. These may be solutions outside the marketing or advertising realm. Your clients turn to you in this role because of trust and loyalty and they turn to you first.

3. *Educator or information provider.* With the speed of change, our clients—both internal and external—need to be educated. You can be an invaluable resource for your clients by position-ing yourself as an educator and an information provider. The discount clothing retailer, Syms, has a great motto by which we should conduct busi-ness: *An educated consumer is our best customer!*

4. *Communication enhancer.* This is also

referred to as communication facilitator or communication reinforcer. Perhaps your clients simply need you to listen, or perhaps your product or service will help them with their communication challenges.

Now for the lead and the most important role. It's that of *Questioner.*

We must constantly ask ourselves, "What business am I really in?". I hate to be the one to break the news to you, but most of you are under the influence of some type of business-induced trance! Most of you are having hallucinations! I don't believe that the majority of your answers would be the purpose of your business. None describe what you *really* do for a living.

I think the purpose of all of our businesses is simply to *attain and retain customers.* If you don't create and keep customers, tomorrow you won't have a business. Agreed?

What would happen if you stopped looking at your primary role in

your business, as the provider of ideas? If you don't have customers for whom to provide those ideas and if the ideas don't work for the customers, it won't do you any good. What would happen if you looked at your emerging lead role as becoming a *Customer Attaining and Retaining Agent?* When you think about it this way, several things happen. First of all, you aren't tied to a specific product or service because all you are doing is creating customers and continually filling their needs.

Thus, you have five roles. The main role is the customer creating and retaining agent. The supporting roles are

1. *Challenge solver*
2. *Solution broker*
3. *Information provider*
4. *Communication Enhancer*

Over the next few days, I would like to ask you to really delve into how you can take on each of these new roles in your businesses or *your* professional life.

#3 Learn to Listen to the Environment for Whispers of Possibility

Listen to ideas that your environment offers you. When you think about environmental factors that influence your business, you may think of technology, change, diversity, economy, natural disaster, aging of America, pollution, government control, crime, downsizing and so on. But look at these factors from a different perspective. Within each environmental challenge is an opportunity somewhere. You know, if the dinosaurs were able to do an accurate environmental survey, they may be around today! Dinosaur companies who are unable to analyze their environment and look for opportunities within it, face the same fate as the dinosaurs. We have to ask ourselves, what environmental factors have I been complaining about or ignoring that could present a real opportunity to create and retain new clients?

#4 Learn to Think in New Ways

Why is it important for an Olympic athlete to practice every day? To get better at it! We seem to take the basics for granted. How many people practice thinking in new ways as a real discipline? Very few. One of the reasons much of our world is in a quandary as to how to solve our many challenges, is because of this inability to think in a new way. Einstein said "Everything has changed except our ways of thinking." We have to apply the same disciplines in getting ourselves to think in new ways as we do to getting our bodies into shape or in learning to play a musical instrument.

So this fourth step in learning to see the invisible, is to make opportunity-finding a habit every day.

Henry Ford said "Thinking is the most difficult work in the world and that's why so few people ever do it." Most of us are thinking the same thoughts in the same way every day and that's why we may beat ourselves up for never having an original thought when we really need one. That's because we don't PRACTICE THINKING.

I have been driven in my passion to find out why people perceive the world—or the same challenges—in ways that limit us unnecessarily. I have been on this quest in trying to discover how it is that we can practice seeing challenges in new ways...consciously, so that it becomes a habitual, systematic resource upon which we can call at any time to see the invisible. So far, I have discovered that there is one secret at the core of being able to think in new ways. One secret at the core of all innovation. One secret at the core of all creative genius. Every creative or innovative idea is the answer to one or more questions asked consciously or unconsciously. Therefore, you can learn to create ideas at will, by learning to ask yourself the right questions on a habitual basis. It doesn't mean that we will all become creative geniuses. I do believe that we all have some natural talents over each other. Some of you are more naturally athletic than others and some are more naturally talented in music or math. But we can dramatically increase our creativity and innovative power by asking the right kinds of questions on a regular basis... simply questioning the norm.

Six Questions for Opportunity Finding

If you apply these questions every single day in every aspect of your world, you find that eventually, (and this is a gradual progression-it doesn't happen overnight-it requires some discipline) you can begin to see the invisible...to even see Harvey!

Here are the questions:

1. What are the emerging industries, markets and opportunities in *my* area of expertise?

2. What are the greatest frustrations or challenges that the people in these emerging markets are facing or going to face?

3. What are their most pressing internal and external needs?

4. How can what I do help?

5. What else is needed to solve this challenge?

6. How can I position myself or my company as an essential challenge-solving resource in this industry?

This process looks deceptively simple, but I challenge you to go through these questions every day for the next twenty-one days and I will guarantee you that you will see opportunities that you have never seen before. Brainspark (the act of sparking ideas versus the violence of brainstorming) with other people outside of your area of expertise. Read books about things you normally wouldn't read. Go to trade shows that you have no reason to attend. If you subscribe to *Mother Jones*, subscribe to *National Review*. Stretch your mind in all these different ways because the more you do that, you will find that creative genius is a matter of taking disparate ideas and putting them together.

The final step in the Harvey Principle may seem like an afterthought, but it is in fact, the most important.

#5 Learn How to Connect the Dots

There's an old Chinese proverb that says, "If you want one year of prosperity, grow grain. If you want 10 years of prosperity, grow trees. If you want a lifetime of prosperity, *grow people!*"

Ultimately, the success and profitability of your organization is only as good as the people in it. If you aren't helping those people to grow, if you are not constantly learning and growing; if you aren't caring and compassionate to your people; then ultimately you can't win the game.

You commit to connecting the dots when you commit to the development of everyone with whom you come in contact.

You commit to connecting the dots when you make a total commitment to absolute gender equality within your workplace. You commit to connecting the dots when you commit to keeping ethics above all else.

You commit to connecting the dots when you take care of yourself mentally, physically, spiritually and yes, financially.

You commit to connecting the dots when you commit to nurturing human potential in all aspects of your business.

I want you to take a few minutes over the next couple of days and ask yourself, "How can I bring more caring, compassion and character into every aspect of my professional life?" This will get you started on your commitment to connecting the dots.

I want to share a poem with you that I wrote, loosely based on one called *Threads* written by James Autry. Mine is called Connecting the Dots.

Connecting the Dots

Sometimes you just connect with an internal or external client...in an instant.

No big thing maybe, but something beyond just marketing and selling the same old product or service...

It comes and goes quickly so you have to pay attention.

A change in the eyes when you ask about their family, a pain flickering behind the statistics about their boy or girl in school far from home.

An older colleague talks about his bride with affection after 25 years.

A hot-eyed achiever laughs before you want him to.

Someone tells about his wife's job and how proud he is of her.

A woman says she spends a lot of salary on a day care and a good one's hard to find, but worth it.

LISTEN! LISTEN AND CONNECT THE DOTS!

In every conversation with your clients, you hear the dots of love, the dots of joy, the dots of fear and guilt, the cries of celebration and re-assurance and somehow we know that connecting those dots is what we are supposed to do and business will take care of itself.

If It Is Broke, Don't Fix It...Yet

Stop Trying to Solve Your Clients' Challenges Too Quickly

I recently read the book by John Grey, *Men are from Mars, Women are from Venus.* I have to admit that it wasn't because I was particularly interested in better understanding my relationship with my wife, but because it was presented to me by my mate as a "wonderful tool in my business." Either way, she got me to read it.

The overt message of the book is that men and women speak different languages. Men speak Martian and women speak Venusian. Whether or not you have read the book, you know this to be true. My wife arrives home and exclaims, "This house is a mess!" What's she really saying? "This house is a mess!" But, what do I hear? "Did you make this mess, you slob? Pick up this stuff before I get really angry!" It's that guilt thing guys!

But there is an underlying message in this book that really got me pondering the creative process in any small business. That message is that *men won't listen.* Unfortunately, we males also know this to hold true. We want to fix things; it's just our nature. A woman, on the other hand, just wants us to listen. A while ago, my wife came home from work looking frustrated and explained that she had just experienced "the worst week of work in her entire life." Without hesitation I looked at her as empathetically as I could and said "Quit!" As if that wasn't bad enough, I was dumb enough to follow this with, "What's for dinner?" Not the makings of strong communications in any relationship.

I'd like to write a book called, *Business Professionals are from Mars. Everyone Else is from Venus.* Because of the nature of the entre-preneurial beast, we have been trained to fix things. In a recent workshop, I asked small busi-ness owners what was one benefit they offered their clients. 90% of respondents said that they are in the business of solving their clients' problem...of fixing things.

Rumor has it that the leading manufacturer of typewriters back in the 1880's was approached

by Remington Inc. to sell their company.
Remington, however, commented that it would not
make an offer until the original company solved a
serious problem that had been uncovered.

Remington had discov-
ered that typists were
complaining that the
keys of the
typewriter
were sticking.

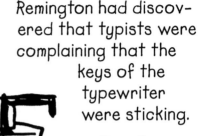

Now, I remem-
ber not too long
ago, having to
reach in and undo
stuck typewriter
keys, so it must
have been a lot
worse back at the turn of the century. Keep in
mind that the keyboard configuration did not
look anything like it does today. In this instance,
the top row was capitals, the second row was
small letters, the next was numbers and the
bottom row was punctuation. Finally, the letters
were arranged alphabetically and the keys were
about double the size they are now.

The president of the original company got his
bigwigs together and challenged them to solve
the problem. To their credit, they did not jump to
the solution too quickly. They did something that
hits at the very core of creativity and is *my*

motto in business today. "When you have a problem, BLAME THE CUSTOMER!" Now, don't do this out loud, but it truly helps to take the blame off of your people and put it elsewhere. So, the typewriter executives said, "It's not our fault the typewriter keys stick. It's the typist's fault—they're typing too quickly." From this, the company's engineers came up with the most inefficient keyboard system they could dream of. It's called QWERTY (the first six letters of your keyboard) and we still live with it today.

Think about it. The I and the O are the third and sixth most frequently used letters in the English language. Where are they located? Top right and probably your weakest fingering. The new configuration did slow down typists and the company was sold to Remington! I don't want you to rebel against typewriters, but I also want you to hesitate before you just try to fix your clients' challenges. Maybe we need to re-evaluate the problem before jumping to the solution too soon. By doing this, we set ourselves apart from our competition by exhibiting more professionalism and innovation.

Step Into My Office

Shattering the Stereotype of Doing Business With You

I was driving my rental car along Northwest Highway in Dallas. I had about three hours to kill prior to my scheduled flight. I turned a corner and there in front of me was a building with a sign, "DALLAS FINE CARS... Luxury Automobiles at Their Best."

I have never taken time to stop to look at these high-priced indulgences. I hear this mid-life crisis thing is coming, so my wife tells me it's OK to look at sports cars...as long as that's all I do!

I pulled into the parking lot, got out of my car and peered through the window of the show-room. There, in the middle of the floor (on a pedestal), was the biggest, the blackest, the most beautiful Mercedes Benz I have ever seen in my entire life. At that moment, all I wanted to do was sit behind the wheel of that car and fantasize that I owned it.

Before I go any further, do we have a stereotype of the "typical" car salesperson? Absolutely! You may be married to one. You may have had a great experience with one, but overall, we still have a vision of the stereotypical car salesperson in North America. I am aware that many car companies are working on this image, but the fact remains that this impression is still not a good one.

Adjectives such as sleezy, slick, dishonest, aggressive, pushy and Herb Tarlick still roll off of most peoples' tongues. I have the same stereotype plus the amazing realization that this is the one industry with whom I have conducted sales training, in which they can't sell you their product! Ask a car salesperson for their card. Their title is likely to be "Sales Associate" or "Salesperson". Then you get to the point when you want to buy the car and they panic... "Oh, wait! I have to get my sales manager." They can't sell it to you!

So, I have the same stereotype as most others as I push open the door of the car dealership. Before I could even get through the doorframe, my stereotype was completely shattered. Why?

A woman approached me. Now, I would venture to guess that even if you are a woman, you wouldn't have thought of a woman when I asked you to stereotype the typical car salesperson. We think of a man.

This was great. My stereotype was completely shattered as a woman approached...but she didn't let me down. You can guess the first words out of her mouth. In any retail situation, what do we get asked the most? "Can I help you?" And, what is our defensive answer—whether we mean it or not? "No thanks. Just looking."

This is a pet peeve of mine. If you have any responsibility over this in your business, think of something besides asking, "Can I help you?" It's like getting your swords out. Imagine two people facing each other. The first yells, "Can I help you?" while drawing their sword. In response, the second waves his sword while proclaiming, "No thanks. Just looking." Not to be daunted, dueler #1 jabs his sword while asking, "What can I show you today?" In a final display of showmanship, dueler #2 strikes back with "Nothing! I am just looking." OK. Maybe I get carried away, but that's just how bad I think it is to ask this meaningless question.

Back to the car dealership...when we had last left our hero (me), I had just begun jousting and had sternly reported that I was just there to look. Without another word, the woman looked me in the eye and ordered, "Step into my office!"

I thought I was hearing things. I could of sworn she had just ordered me into her office. I was still standing in the doorframe. The look on my face must have betrayed my confusion. Without hesitation, she repeated, "Step into my office," as she turned her back and walked away.

I am a sales trainer, but I don't need another case history. After the shock wore off, I decided it was time to hightail it out of there. As I turned to leave, I glanced over my shoulder one more time. Do you know what she had done? She had walked swiftly to the back door of that black, Mercedes Benz—at which she must have seen me looking in the window when I first arrived. She opened the back door of the car, slid into the back seat and, with a smile on her face, she now yelled at me—through two open doors—"Step into my office!"

I was back! Oh, come on. It's been a long time since I was in the back seat of a car with a woman. And, my wife will tell you, it was never a Mercedes Benz!

How odd is this? I now find myself sitting in the back seat of the car with this salesperson, when she barks another order. "Shut the door." I comply.

Without hesitation (and I have now totally given over control to her), my new friend looks at me mischievously and tells me to smell. Not sure that I heard her correctly, I ask her to repeat the command. She repeated, "Smell."

"Shouldn't we introduce ourselves first?" I try to stall.

"Just smell." She is getting impatient.

As I take in what I can using my olfactory senses, I find myself overwhelmed with the smell of leather. I relate this to the young woman.

"That's what your kids are going to smell when they are sitting in these seats," she explains.

All I could say was a very profound "WOW." She had me now.

Next, she asked me to look around the front seat and report what I saw. I observed a leather-bound steering wheel and wood paneling. When I was done reporting, she explained, "That's what your kids are going to see when you are driving this car!"

Again, all I could utter was, "WOW!"

"Sir, do you like to go fast?" she teased. "Yeah, really fast," I mumbled. "This car is the fastest car on the lot," she explained boastfully.

Another "WOW".

Next came an invitation. "Imagine your hand on that stick shift; shifting from fourth into fifth at eighty to eighty-five miles an hour."

"WOW"

Then came the kicker. "Do you have the money?"

"No," I replied honestly.

"Bye."

It completely shattered the stereotype of the *experience* I expected to have walking in those doors.

Do your clients have a stereotype of the experience they are going to have with you? Whether it's an internal client or an external client, we must constantly figure out ways to shatter the stereotypes that they have of us, our product or service, or of doing business with us. Perhaps it's physically changing the environment or surroundings. Maybe it means holding that weekly meeting in a different venue. You could simply change your voice mail message.

Do whatever it takes to first, understand the stereotypes that exist in your business and then to shatter them...creatively!

The Two Most Powerful Words...

How to Get "Buy In" Once You Are Creative

Let me introduce you to the two most powerful words when it comes to creativity-in-business. To tease you a little, when we first discovered these words in our business many years ago, they accounted for a 37% increase in business in one year. Not only that, but they eventually changed the way we interacted with our internal and external clients; they illustrated how to get "buy in" to our creative ideas. And, finally, these two words changed the way I parent my children as well.

Curious? The two words are "what if." Allow me to take you through a series of what-iffing that changed the way we did business.

At its very basic level, what-iffing "shatters the stereotype of the experience your clients expect to have with you." (see previous chapter). I must give credit to one of my creativity gurus, Roger von Oech. He is the author of a wonderful book, first published by Warner Books in 1983, *A Whack On The Side of the Head*. In 1986 he published a sequel, *A Kick In The Seat of the Pants* through Harper and Row Publishing. Both are tremendous books on the whole creative process. Von Oech introduces his readers to What Iffing. I took his suggestion, and began by starting all of my staff meetings with this concept.

Appoint someone, the "What-if-questioner" of the day. Their job is to come prepared to kick off the meeting with a bizarre, unreal and totally un-work-related What If question. For example, "What if humans didn't need to sleep?" "What if we had a twelve-year-old President or Prime Minister?" A client of mine recently tried this and the question was, "What if hair grew inward instead of out?" I have to clear my throat just thinking about it!

Once the question is on the table, go around the room and make everyone answer it. What's going to happen? One-the creative juices will start flowing and you will be amazed at what comes out. Two-anyone who doesn't normally contribute will be thinking, "Wow, anything I say couldn't be nearly as weird as what just went on here!" And, three-your people will start to have FUN! Wouldn't you agree with me that people want to work for/work with people who seem to enjoy what they do for a living? As a matter of fact, in all of my consulting, I have discovered a very simple principle...

There is a direct correlation between the amount of fun an organization encourages and the amount of creative breakthroughs that organization experiences.

People are more likely to contribute in an environment that is fun, creative and innovative than in one that is the "same old, same old."

There is one last saying that should be imprinted in your brain. This is one of those sayings that I have used as my personal creativity reminder for years, but one which I have no idea to whom I owe credit.

There is very little difference between "aha" and "ha-ha"

Then, once you have mastered this internally, try it with your external clients as well. A national financial services firm, with whom I have worked, embraced What iffing whole-heartedly. Their financial planners now start their initial, prospective client meetings with What If. Imagine this:

(Planner) "What if you had $2,000,000.00 under your mattress right now?"

(Prospect) Really? OK. First, I would want to put enough away to take care of my aging parents. Also, I would want to make sure that my kids' education was covered. Then, I would quit my job and take my husband around the world—twice!"

What's just happened? As odd as this sounded, it shattered the stereotypical presentation that the prospect expected. More important, whether the prospect has two million dollars or two thousand dollars, they have just expressed their financial priorities, their hopes and their dreams.

Let's take what-iffing to the next level. Imagine if you will, that you now work for me. Let's also suppose that you get to work every morning around 9 a.m. I come to you one day and state, "We have this huge proposal that we have to get done. I can't finish it without your input. I know you normally get here at 9 a.m, but I want you here by 7 a.m. tomorrow."

How would that make you feel? Not very tactful, was it? But, that is basically the way I worked with my people when I first started in business. I thought it was normal—in business—for people to come to work for me for thirty days and leave!

Then, I discovered what if. Imagine the same scenario: "Hey, you are a huge part of the team and I can't do this proposal without you. I know you normally get here at nine o'clock, but *what if* you came in at seven o'clock tomorrow and get it done?"

At this point, I want to teach you a very sophisticated creativity-in-business concept called "B.Y.T" or *bite your tongue!* I can't tell you how many people, with whom I have worked, who ask a question and then answer it. If you ask a question, shut up and listen.

(Employee) "Jeff, I can't get here by seven because I can't get my kids to the babysitter before seven-fifteen. That means I couldn't be here until at least seven-forty-five."

(Jeff) "Could you get here every day this week at seven-forty-five?"

(Employee) "Sure. And, if I don't get it done, I could come in Saturday morning..."

What just happened? I opened up a dialogue. A dialogue that I didn't allow to exist before because of my management style.

I thought, "If this works at my office, this will surely work at home."

We use a disciplinary tactic in our home called "time out". Many of you are probably familiar with this strategy. (My parents think we are out of our minds. "Just hit the kid" is more their approach to child rearing!) About the time that I discovered "What If", I realized how threatening

I must have sounded to my three year old. "Get into time out and figure out why you did what you just did." Not much room for discussion.

To this day, no matter how angry I am with my girls, I always start with What If. "What if you went into your room and figured out why you just hit your little sister?" In their minds, it is less-threatening and it opens up a dialog (not that I would listen to a word they say when I'm really angry!). In fact, now that my oldest daughter is almost sixteen, she won't hesitate to start the dialog, "I'll tell you why I did i." And we have this amazing conversation that just blows me away. Why? Because when you open up a dialog, you had better be prepared for what you are about to hear.

Finally, let me tie this together by showing you how we made money with What If. I recall a sunny day in 1983, when I returned to a prospect's office to make a creative presentation. Part of my advertising business was devoted to promotional products. This client had given me the challenge of coming up with an imprinted item that would attract people to their trade show booth at various shows around the country. Let me paraphrase the conversation as I recall it...

(Jeff) "Thanks for meeting with me about your trade show challenge. We spent some time brainstorming, and we think you should give away ceramic coffee mugs."

Interested nod from prospect encouraged me to continue.

(Jeff) "We can put your fifteen-color logo on one side and your mission statement on the other. When people come into your booth, fill the mug with water. Attendees will be walking around the show with a cup of water and others will inquire as to where they got it. What do you think?"

(Prospect) "Great idea, Jeff. What else did you come up with?"

(Jeff) "You don't understand. I have been in this business for nine years and I know that this is the answer."

In this scenario, how do we sell our ideas? Like two fists hammering each other and, if I hit hard enough, I win. Now, let's look at the same scenario using what if.

(Jeff) "Thanks for meeting with me about your trade show challenge. What if you gave away ceramic coffee mugs?" B.Y.T! Stop and listen.

(Prospect) "Jeff, I can't. I can't ship ceramic across the country because they will break."

(Jeff) "What if we used plastic mugs?"

(Prospect) "Hey, what if we used plastic beer

steins? Our theme this year is 'Flow Through Ideas' and a beer stein might get the point across."

(Jeff) "I have a plastic beer stein that, when you put cold water in it, the imprint changes color."

(Prospect) "What if we imprinted it with our old logo and our new logo appeared...?"

Back and forth. Back and forth. When I leave, what does the prospect say to everyone with whom they work? "*I* have a great idea and I want to work with Jeff because it feels right."

We need to check our egos at the door. I wasn't trying to pull the wool over this person's eyes. I truly believed that ceramic coffee mugs were the "right" answer to her challenge of what to give away in the tradeshow booth. But, if she doesn't believe it, it doesn't matter what I think. I walked in selling ceramic coffee mugs. I walked out selling plastic beer steins. Why? Because I opened up a dialogue and somewhere in that repartee, we both agreed that plastic beer steins just might be the second right answer to the challenge of what to give away.

In a previous chapter I said, "As long as your client uses the tools you give them, and the goal doesn't change, who cares how you get there?" As long as she uses the tools I give her and the goal—what do I give away in my tradeshow booth—doesn't change, who cares how we get there?

That's the power of what-iffing. The results don't come without risk. By opening up a dialogue with your clients, you had better be prepared for where you may go.

To Err is Right...or at Least Necessary

Taking the Fear Out of The Creative Process

Most business people are not comfortable with mistakes. We learn early that it is good to be right and bad to be wrong. These values are all a result of our educational system, which–when you think about it-rewards us by grading the number of right and wrong answers and teaches us that we will be rewarded in life for being right and will have limited opportunities if we make mistakes.

The notion of not being able to make mistakes is still evident in every facet of our adult lives. There are few people who are willing to admit their mistakes in a very public arena. We tend to take risks only on a private level where we feel safe.

This attitude makes sense in many circumstances. You wouldn't want your stockbroker to be wrong too many times. You would assume that the engineer did not make too many mistakes when designing the bridge you drive over every morning. And, every time you board an airplane, you are betting that the pilot is not overly comfortable with making too many errors.

When it comes to the business of selling, however, TO ERR IS NOT WRONG! Mistakes are a necessary bi-product of the creative process. If you are willing to accept the norm because that is the way it's always been done, if you are prepared to sell the same old product or service because it's an old mainstay, then you are not exercising your "risk muscle" and your creative genius can only be stifled.

As Benjamin Franklin once said, "The man who does things makes many mistakes, but he never makes the biggest mistake of all—doing nothing!"

One of the biggest reasons we don't tend to take risks when confronted with the many challenges we face is *fear.* Fear keeps us from turning that "one-in-a-million" idea into reality. Fear is the greatest hindrance to successful risk-taking and to performing our best under pressure. To keep ahead of change and to successfully confront the many challenges we face in business, we need to learn how to overcome this obstacle.

The good news about the fear of failure is that we have plenty of company. Everyone is afraid when taking a risk or tackling a new challenge. If you say you have no fears, you are either playing life much too safely or you just are not in touch with your own feelings.

"Heroes and cowards feel exactly the same fear," said Gus D'Amato, the great boxing trainer to such prize fighters as Floyd Patterson and Mike Tyson. But like all champions, D'Amato adds, "Heroes just react to fear differently."

Fear is like a wall that limits your view and creates boundaries to your growth and especially to your innate creativity. The creative person recognizes that the breakthroughs in their own creative genius, learning and growth, lie beyond the wall.

To get over the fear of failure, you must first acknowledge it. There is an old American Indian story that says fear is like a sixty-foot, two-headed snake as big around as a large tree. Avoid it and the snake grows larger and comes closer, rearing its huge ugly head, ready to strike. But, if you look the snake in the eye, it sees its own reflection, gets scared and slithers away. The next time you face a challenge that requires you to take the risk that you might be wrong—that you might fail—stand up to your two-headed snake of fear.

One entrepreneur with whom I worked, stated that he felt that true risk-taking is for those who have the time and money to do so. Wrong! The truth is, we are all born risk takers. How else do we learn to walk, talk, ride a bike, ski or get ourselves into business?

I am not a scientist, but I would venture to guess that research would show that we learn more in the first decade of our lives than we ever will after that. That's no accident. Isn't this the period that we are more likely to take risks?

If we weren't born risk takers, we would all be crawling around on our hands and knees! "I don't know if I should try to stand. I'm only one-year-old. I will fall. I think I will wait until I am older and stronger." As children, we don't know any better than to explore the unknown, the untried, the untested every day. This is the prime time for making mistakes, picking ourselves up, dusting ourselves off, and trying again!

It should become evident that you can't learn without taking risks. It's the way we have mastered everything. Growth and creativity come from trial and error. As Lloyd Jones noted, "The men who try to do something and fail are infinitely better than those who try to do nothing and succeed."

86 the Onions

We Need to Stop Being
So Critical of Our Own Ideas

In discussing creativity with many entrepreneurs around the country, I have found a real need to get back to basics in working with the "internal client" in brainstorming new and innovative approaches to their specific industry.

I would like to clear up some misconceptions about the very word, "brainstorm". I have never felt comfortable with this terminology. We are all familiar with one definition of the word, 'storm' which is an atmospheric disturbance of some kind. Perhaps this is not far off for some people's minds, but I don't think that this is what lexicologists had in mind. I think they were referring to the definition of storm as "a violent outburst" "to attack or assault". Perhaps it's the non-violent being inside me, but this seems a little extreme. For our purposes, I would like to consider ways to "BRAINSPARK". Simply put, we are in search of methods and techniques to spark that part of our brain which will ultimately help us develop new approaches to old challenges.

Every time you sit down to brainspark, force the group to come up with at least thirty-three different options! Thirty-three different ideas? You don't have the time? Where are you going to find other people with whom to brainspark? How do you do this if you can only come up with ten? Relax!

Human nature prevents us from having an open mind all of the time. We tend to play our own worst critic. If you have ever worked in a restaurant, you are aware of the term "86". You may have heard the short order cook screaming, "Order's up! Burger deluxe, 86 the onions". It simply means to "get rid of" or "scratch". It's no different in our business lives. We tend to "86" our ideas before they ever have a chance to develop. This is the first reason to force yourself to come up with at least 33 different ideas when brainstorming. We don't have time to 86 our ideas.

At the risk of making you a little schizophrenic, I like to think that we all walk around with two little, make-believe "beings" on our shoulders. On one side we have our internal Artist whispering things like, "Go for it... Give it a try... What if...". On the other shoulder is our internal Judge whispering in the other ear, "Don't take the risk... You're an idiot to try it... But, it's never been done before." The problem is that too many of us end up listening to our Judge before our artist ever has a chance to finish playing. When it comes to brainsparking for innovative approaches to our challenges, we have to allow the Artist inside to play with the ideas rather than "86ing" them.

I first discovered this concept while working as an outside consultant to an architectural design firm in Singapore. One of my challenges was to see if we could come up with a simple name for a small fabric company that the firm was starting as a sideline. While conducting a two-day program with the group of ten on a variety of creativity and vision issues, just before the lunch break on day one, I asked everyone to bring back suggestions of a new name for this company.

When we reconvened after our meal, I brought out my felt tip pen and positioned my flipchart ready to record a series of great suggestions. What I heard instead was ten individual ideas, one per person, even though I hadn't set any limits. All were similar to the company's current name or, even worse, a competitor's. At first, I prevailed on the group to come up with just one more suggestion and with a little struggle, someone did. Better? Yes, but not nearly good enough.

After a few minutes of consideration, I decided to start the process over again with the rule that now the first eleven names were considered off-limits. So I gave everyone a few minutes and asked for a second series of ten. With some struggling we achieved our goal. Now, I challenged the group to find the eleventh and they did. This was the best of the group.

At the end of the day, I assigned the task of coming up with a third group of ten. After all, they would have all night to think about it. Sure enough, next morning we had ten new names although a few were a bit bizarre. What I learned is what it takes to stretch the mind so that a "brainspark" turns into new and creative solutions. The first ten are easy—the eleventh requires effort. The first round is painless, the second is a challenge and the third demands expansion into new territory. That's how we get to thirty-three – 10 + 1 x 3!

An easy way to understand the reasoning behind the "rule of 33" is to think of it as a road trip to a destination where you've never been before. The first one-third of your trip will be very comfortable—after all, it is territory you already know—your driveway, your neighborhood and your city. The second one-third may not be quite as familiar but it will likely not represent any unusual challenge—perhaps it is across your own state where you have traveled before. It is the last one-third, to the place where you haven't ever been before, the uncharted territory that represents the unknown, that presents the challenge. This road can be the most exciting part of the trip—so don't stop until you get there. And don't stop brainsparking until you get to the place you've not explored yet.

Keep in mind that creativity is a one-on-one sport and innovation is a team sport. Allow your team members to come up with ideas, but remember that it takes the entire team to implement them.

House on Wheels

Get Outside Your Comfort Zone to Find Answers

On a dreary day in November, I found myself reading the Sunday newspaper when I came across a full-page, full-color advertisement for the Recreational Vehicle Show coming to my hometown of Pittsburgh. Please don't be offended but, I tease people who dream of retiring and "seeing the country" in an R.V., by asking them why in the  world they would want to carry their houses on their backs. Just not my dream!

My advertising background made me more interested in the obvious expense this show went to for this advertisement. I turned the newspaper towards my wife who was sitting opposite me on the sofa.

"Look at this," I explained. "What a waste of advertising!"

I did not even get the newspaper turned back around before my wife retorted, "Excuse me?"

"What?" I asked.

"Oh, Mr. Creativity himself. Isn't it you that tells people to get outside of their comfort zones and try things a little different?" she challenged.

I just nodded my head and she ordered, "Go!"

"Go where?" I asked.

"Go to the R.V. show"

"I am NOT going to the R.V. show!" I declared.

When I was at the R.V. show...I was immediately enraptured by the 'toys' I found there! I was so impressed that the following summer, I rented a thirty-two foot R.V. in Calgary, Alberta and took my family on a ten-day adventure through the Canadian Rockies. It was the most incredible trip of our lives. All because I forced myself—OK! I was forced—to go to the R.V. show!

Many of the answers to the challenges we face in our lives do not lie within the "four walls" of our lives. We need to constantly and consciously force ourselves to do some things that are very uncomfortable to be more creative.

THOUGHTS ON...

Marketing

A Modern Fairy Tale

See the World Through Your Clients' Eyes and Change Your Perspective

Allow me to relate a modern fairy tale. It takes place in a land with a very deep and fast flowing river running right through the middle. No one is able to cross the river by themselves, without drowning. On one side of the river, we find Miss A. On the other side of the river, Mr. B. Now, over time Miss A and Mr. B have developed quite a relationship by just talking across the river. It occurs to them that they are deeply in love. But, the river poses quite an obstacle. One day, Miss A turns to Mr. B and, professing her love, she asks him to stay put while she walks down the levee to try to find a way across. Not far away, Miss A comes upon Mr. C, who has a boat. Passionate about getting across the river, she explains her dilemma to Mr. C and asks him to ferry her so that she can be with her true love.

Mr. C agrees to take Miss A across the river–if she will kiss him. Miss A is taken aback and refuses to kiss Mr. C because of her love for Mr. B. Mr. C simply restates his 'price', only to be rejected once more. Distraught, Miss A trudges further along the riverbank. Soon she encounters Mr. D! Mr. D is sitting in a rocking chair minding his own business when Miss A approaches. She explains the whole situation and she begs for Mr. D's assistance. Mr. D refuses! He explains, in no uncertain terms, that he doesn't want to get involved. He feels that this is none of his business and he asks Miss A to leave him alone.

Feeling defeated, Miss A decides to exercise her only viable option as she treks back to Mr. C and acquiesces to his demands. True to his word, Mr. C takes Miss A across the river in his boat. Miss A makes her way along the other side of the river, soon to be in the arms of her true love.

As she approaches Mr. B, he calls out to her, asking her to explain how she got there. Miss A tells him the whole sordid story leaving no stone unturned. After listening to all of this and without hesitation, Mr. B turns to Miss A and informs her that he doesn't want her anymore. He explains that his standards are very clear and, since she kissed Mr. C, he could no longer accept her!

Confused and forlorn, Miss A trudges along the riverbank without any idea of what to do. Suddenly she comes across Mr. E! Mr. E is on a horse—a white horse—and he is dressed in white. After Miss A explains the whole situation, Mr. E only takes a second to consider the situation. He explains to Miss A that he doesn't care about her past and that he loves her just the way she is. He invites her to join him on his horse as they ride off into the sunset together. She does! They do! End of story.

After you have put your tissues away, if I were to ask you to rate our five characters according to how much you respect them, how do you think your list would look? Perhaps you would put Miss A at the top because of her stamina, her perseverance or her tenaciousness. Perhaps she would be at the bottom of your list because she compromised herself. Did you respect Mr. B the most because he was principled? Or perhaps the least because he was inflexible? Maybe Mr. C would top your list because he had a price and stuck to it or he could be at the bottom because he was obviously an opportunist. Did you respect Mr. D because of his ability to stay uninvolved or perhaps you didn't like the fact that he would not help a damsel in distress! Finally, maybe you put Mr. E at the top of your column; the knight in shining armor, able to accept our heroine no matter what her past. Or is Mr. E really the opportunist in this story?

The point is that these are all right. The word that should come to mind is *perspective.* The ability to understand that in any given situation, someone else may have a totally different perspective of the same information. Recognize that world class marketers always take this into account. They see the world through their market's eyes, allowing them to see the way their market buys. The next time you send out that direct mail piece, the next time you give away that promotional product, stop and consider your clients' perspective—not yours!

What This Means To You Is...

The Real Scoop on Benefits Versus Features in Your Business

In my capacity as a sales and marketing consultant, I often like to travel with some outside representatives of any company with which I am about to work. It is an eye-opening experience when you have no vested interest in the outcome of the call and you can truly sit back and listen to the exchange. Oh sure, I want them to succeed, but I am interested more in the reaction of their prospects.

Recently, I spent the day with a woman from a large promotional products company on the west coast. Rhonda was a little nervous as she knew that this experience might be put under a microscope when the entire company convened the next day for training. Yet, the owner of the firm had assured me that Rhonda was the most professional and successful representative that they had working in the field. I tried to assuage her fears by guaranteeing that I was not there to be a critic, but rather to observe.

Now, Rhonda had spent an enormous amount of time and energy in preparing a power point presentation to WOW potential clients. I was immediately impressed at how prepared she was going into our first meeting of the day with a committee who was to decide about a new safety program for their factory. Rhonda was professional to a tee and her ability to relate to all of the personalities in the room was envious.

As the slide show began, I could feel the anticipation in the room because this group had obviously not been treated to this level of professionalism in the past. The first slide showed a graphic of Rhonda's company logo. Cascading into the frame was a large bullet point, "Since 1892". She explained that her firm, ABC Company (the names have been changed to protect the innocent!), had been in business since 1892. The next bullet to appear simply read, "Largest" and she offered that ABC Company was the largest distributor of its kind on the west coast. As the third bullet appeared, I looked around the room to looks of various levels of interest. One gentleman had begun doodling on his notepad and a woman opposite me was giving one of those continuous nods of agreement.

When Rhonda finished fifteen minutes later, there were some courteous questions and we were dismissed. As we approached her car, Rhonda looked at me and asked what she had done wrong. She said that she knew that she didn't get the account because she had not "clicked" with the committee. I was stumped, but I knew that she had not held their interest.

As we drove to the next presentation, it hit me. I always contend that your clients only listen to one radio station around the world—WIIFM (What's In It For Me!). They don't care that you have been in business for 1000 years and that you are the best in the world. They want to know how that translates to a benefit for them.

I offered a solution to Rhonda. "What if—in this next call—you give the exact same presentation, but every time you give one of your bulleted points, you offered two benefits to the group?"

After considering this challenge, Rhonda agreed but interrogated me further as to how she could do that. I explained that there is a very simple formula to ensure that one always keeps the benefits in mind. Every time you offer a response—a feature—follow it up with some form of the words, "what this means to you is...". Then, when you finish this, you repeat, "what this also means to you is...".

Rhonda agreed to try it.

The next meeting was with only two people looking for the perfect giveaways for an upcoming company-wide picnic. The presentation began. The first bullet appeared and Rhonda started her monologue.

"We have been in business since 1892. What this means to you is that you will be working with a well—established company—not a fly-by-night. What this also means is that, because we have more experience in promotional advertising than any other company in the area, we have more resources to offer our clients." Not bad! Not bad!

The next bullet appeared. *"Largest"*. Rhonda piped in, "We are the largest distributor of our kind on the west coast so we are able to pass on volume discounts to you, saving you money. This also allows you peace of mind in knowing that there is always someone in our office who can help you, even if I am out on the road." *Touché!*

Now, I don't want to brag or anything, but Rhonda got the order on the spot. Her clients loved her presentation which she masterfully had altered with only the words she used.

My challenge to you is to look at what you do for a living. Look at your business. Ask yourself whether or not you are offering benefits at every opportunity you can. When you introduce yourself to someone do you simply tell them what you do (features) or do you tell them what you can do for them (benefits)? When you exhibit at a trade show, does the sign in the back of your booth boast your company name (features) or what your company can do for someone who is interested (benefits).

By the way, Rhonda called me the other day to ask my advice on something else. She asked for advice and continued, "What offering this advice means to you is..."!

Why Different Can Be Good

Re-Creating the Category In Which You Currently Compete

If you are feeling the heat of new competition lately, you are probably doing something right.

A couple of days ago, I was surveying the shelves of my local pharmacy. A summer cold had gotten hold of me. While browsing through all of the latest cold medicines, one caught my attention; "Thera Flu" from Sandoz Pharmaceuticals.

This is not an endorsement for the product, but the name Thera Flu versus all of the others which had "cold" in their name was the attraction. As a matter of fact, upon closer scrutiny, I realized that Thera Flu has the exact same ingredients as most of the other cold remedies. But it's not a cold remedy. It's a flu remedy. In my mind, that put Thera Flu all by itself in a whole new category. This is marketing at a different level.

It occurs to me that successful businesses attract competitors the way sugar draws ants. The more you grow, the more others are thinking about how they can steal away the markets you have built.

One way to stay a step ahead: Change the rules in the middle of the game. That's obviously what Sandoz Pharmaceuticals has done. I can only guess that when me-too competitors started to elbow their way into the long established category of cold remedy medicines, Sandoz figured it may be time to shift gears and create a whole new category. That got them out of the "ours is better than theirs" trap.

I began looking for other companies who have re-created their category. I found a financial services company that positioned itself as the leader in healthcare equipment leasing—even though its "healthcare" leases worked just like any other lease. They were the first in this new category.

What about the first printing firm who declared themselves a "quick printer"? Other printers probably had the same capabilities, but customers in a hurry will go to the quick printer first.

As I became more aware of this marketing ploy, I began to understand that when creative marketers can't continue to create new categories, they still try to change the rules. They simply turn their weaknesses into strengths and their competitors' strengths into weaknesses.

Accentuate your negatives and turn them into positives. If you succeed, the competitor's marketing of your negatives will actually reinforce *your* message. I remember Warner-Lambert marketing Listerine as "the taste you hate twice a day." A perfect example. What about Smuckers—hardly an appetizing name—who boasted, "With a name like Smuckers, it has to be good."?

If this doesn't apply to you, then look at *turning your competitor's strengths into weaknesses.* When a competitor dominates the market because of a unique competency—for example, because it has a patented process—it may think it has a lock on the market. The best example of this? How about "7-Up—The Un-Cola"? These are opportunities waiting to present themselves to you.

Customers hate feeling beholden to a single supplier—no matter how well that supplier treats them. And they may go to surprising lengths to be sure they have other options. I recently worked with a telecommunications company which was researching a new technology that could compete against satellites to carry TV programming. But the technology still needed a lot of expensive research and development. To my surprise, I found that several of the major networks had pitched in to help. Even though they were happy with what they were using, they wanted other options—just in case.

Shift Happens

A Look at Changes as It Relates To Your Mission Statement

Someone once said, "The only person who welcomes change is a wet baby!" As I travel around the country speaking to so many businesses, I have found very strong reactions to change in the arena of marketing. These reactions range from "If it ain't broke, don't fix it" to *If It Ain't Broke...Break It!* (The latter being the title to a great book by author Robert Kriegel!). I tend to agree whole-heartedly with the last attitude. To go to market more creatively, we have to stop looking in the rear-view mirror to see how things have been done in the past, and start looking through the windshield to see what's coming down the road ahead in our specific field!

We tend to blame our "internal clients"—those people with whom we work everyday who are still living in the "dark ages"—but, I propose that if you truly believe that change is inevitable, then be a change-instigator in your organization. The road ahead calls for the leaders to oversee the dismantling of old truths and to prepare people and organizations to deal with, embrace, and to thrive from change, as innovations are proposed, tested, modified—sometimes rejected—and then assimilated. I have heard a lot of lip service paid to an important facet of this thing we call change, but it has almost become an overused cliché. I am referring to your mission statement.

This is not some esoteric, mysterious concept that only the Fortune 500 companies use. Whether you are a "mom-and-pop" operation or a multi-faceted corporation, your company's mission statement is as important to your business as your business plan, your budget or your bottom line. A clear vision of where it is that we truly want our companies to be is only common sense if we are to survive in the 21st century. And guess what? Even this vision statement is constantly changing as your industry changes around us. Your organization needs a vision, a clear under-standing of what it is trying to achieve. The leader's vision includes both the license to dare to be better and the control system that keeps it from deteriorating into directionless anarchy.

Recently, in a brain-sparking session with a large architectural design company in Singapore, we began discussing the ins and outs of having a mission statement. It occurred to me that the concept of a "mission" is often overwhelming, but that there is always a "vision" for the company, whether you ask the receptionist or the managing partners. With this in mind, I encouraged the participants to begin listing their vision of what the company did, who its clients really were and where the company should be in five, ten and twenty years. Then with the vision complete we began to narrow down what we had to a single statement-our mission. The key was to have as many people involved in the "vision-defining" as possible. When it comes to implementing the mission, you will have far more "buy in" if people were involved initially.

Start implementing a mission with action, not a formal declaration. But develop a short "stump speech," stressing examples of people in the ranks living the vision in day-to-day ways. This speech can even be an internal one, but it should inspire, challenge, emphasize improvement and prepare your listeners for the future.

Once they have their vision in place, the most progressive thinkers in this industry are those who realize that though it's important to have an implementation plan, sometimes it's even more important to abandon it! This was best illus-trated to me a few years ago when I had the opportunity to mentally prepare for my first rock climb with Outward Bound in Colorado. Looking up from the bottom, I would mentally plan a route to the top. However, once the climb began, and I progressed a short way up the formation, the view was totally different. From my new vantage point I could see other, more promising routes that were impossible to see from below. So I was constantly changing the route to achieve my goal.

This is no different when it comes to your firm's mission. You must accept the fact that your path to those goals will always be changing—must always be changing. Unlike my climb in Colorado however, you should never really reach the top of your mountain. Your goals and vision should also be constantly changing and improving. It is a well known saying that "success is not a destination, it's a journey." A mission statement is a living thing and will grow with the organization.

In 1971, Bantam published Alvin Toffler's *Future Shock*, which heightened our awareness of the impact of change on our society. Toffler predicted that "millions of ordinary, psychologically normal people will face an abrupt collision with the future...many of them will find it increasingly painful to keep up with the incessant demand for change that characterizes our time."

People tend to resist any idea, behavior or process that threatens their existing beliefs. The message of *Future Shock* upset many because it confronted their present comfort zones. How could such absurd predictions contain any credibility? Yet, such closed-minded responses only reaffirmed the futurist's contention that people may not resist change but we do resist having to change.

A group of Amish people pulled up stakes from their religious settlement in the Midwest and moved to a remote area in Peru. When asked their reason for doing so, one of them responded, "We got tired of having to move our wagons to the side of the road to let the cars go by." They

were, of course, voicing the frustration they felt from being pressured to change. Many people today are fearful of "moving their wagons to the side of the road to let the cars go by."

John Steinbeck was probably right when he suggested, "It is the nature of man as he grows older to protest against change, particularly change for the better."

"There is no such thing as a new idea, only new ways of presenting old ones." When are we going to realize that this holds truer in this industry than in almost any other on the planet? Leon Martel, in his book *Mastering Change, The Key to Business Success*, describes three common traps that keep us from recognizing and using change:

1. Believing that yesterday's solutions will solve today's problems.

2. Assuming present trends will continue.

3. Neglecting the opportunities offered by future change.

Don't get caught in the trap of believing that old ideas, on their own, will succeed in a new market. But if you accept that there are no really new ideas, then you don't have to re-invent the wheel either.

The Sunshine State

Understanding the Four Market Sectors to Whom We Must Appeal

I recently read an article in a magazine by an author whom I admire. He began by superficially describing his surroundings on the beautiful, tropical island of Maui and I immediately lost all respect for him. So, I am pondering whether or not to let you know that I am sitting in the Florida Keys as the Northeast endures another mid-winter northerner.

I am not telling you this to be masochistic, but because the Florida Keys Tourism Board has taught me a very valuable marketing lesson that I must share with you. You see, the only reason I have come to Florida in the recent past is to visit my parents who live here 6 months of the year or because work brings me here. I would never choose to come here for pleasure's sake...until now. My impression is that it is crowded, nobody knows how to drive and the weather is unpredictable. Why go to Florida?

Believe it or not, it was a 60 second commercial I saw on television about four months ago while sitting in my living room watching my favorite football team get pummeled by some other team, that convinced me that marketing works. It was a spoof of the stereotype I had of the Sunshine State. The camera shot was from behind a car, obviously in Miami Beach. All you could see were two hands on the steering wheel and the car gliding along a four lane road (down the center line) at about 15MPH. Then they cut to Daytona Beach where they showed a teenager, sitting atop a van on the beach toasting the camera with a beer in her hand as she simultaneously turned away to vomit over the side. The caption? (paraphrasing...) "The Florida Keys...Unlike What You Would Expect in the Rest of the State." It was funny and it caught my attention and ultimately my pocketbook.

During that same football game, the Florida Keys Tourism Board had another, much shorter advertisement. It showed a man sitting in a hole he had dug on the beach as if he was building sand castles. His wife and children played in the surf as he first waved at them then turned his attention to his building. The camera pans behind him and now displays a laptop and telephone in the hole. The caption? "Nobody Needs To Know You're Still Open For Business...The Florida Keys."

It doesn't sound like a real marketing coup, but I realized what the tourism board had done. Something that is what we call 'the new age of marketing'. No longer can we look at a one-size-fits-all marketing approach in our businesses. As these ads showed me, we must consider that there are four very distinct markets out there. If your advertising, your business' physical environment, your every marketing effort, does not appeal to every one of these styles—either individually or as a group—you are losing out on potential customers.

I have developed nicknames for the four groups of potential clients. You can name them what you like! (Please don't write letters about gender, equality etc. None of these are better than the others. We need all four types to be successful in any business.)

Factoid Fred

Fred wants just the facts. This potential customer simply wants to know the benefit of doing business with you or of using your product or service. They can't be bothered with all of the details. Remember the man building sand castles? This appeals to Factoid Fred because he can get away with his family and still be in touch when he needs to be. He makes quick decisions based on the benefits he perceives that you offer. Fred thrives on a challenge or problem-solving quest. When we market to Fred we must keep it short and to the point. Don't get cutesy and don't waste his time with humorous anecdotes.

Entertain-Me Edna

Edna is the prospect to whom most sales organizations appeal. She likes FUN anyway you can package it. The spoof of the Florida stereo-type appeals to all of your Entertain-Me Ednas because of its lighthearted approach. Like our Factoid Freds, don't bother Edna with details... not because they can't be bothered, but because they are less organized and more likely to forget. Give Edna a cute 800 number that spells out something. Let them know you will take care of the details. Act like their friend and prove to Ednas that, by using the solution you

offer, they will be part of the in-crowd. Impress
Edna with testimonials.

Even Steven

Even Steven likes to know that everything will
go smoothly in using what you are offering. They
are very much team players in their work environment and translate "team" to mean family. When
marketing to Steven, we must consider their family
values and that it is vital to show them why our
solution will help the team/organization. Stevens
require more details than the first two and they
require an upfront plan if things should go
wrong. Steven loves 1-800-HELP lines that are
available 24 hours or a money-back guarantee.
Even Steven is still a people person so don't get
too technical, but ensure him that things will go
evenly.

Detail Doris

This is the sector of the population that most
marketing minds ignore. Doris is so unlike us that
we don't relate and therefore, we isolate this
group. Detail Doris needs just that—DETAILS. Like
our Factoid Freds, they are no-bull, get-down-
to-business types. But unlike Fred, they require
information overload. One of the most effective
means of targeting this group was the final
advertisement I observed on that cold November

day in my living room. The entire commercial-and remember, this is for the beauty of the tropical Florida Keys—simply showed a spreadsheet divided in two. On one side are the *pros* of taking a vacation to the Florida Keys and on the other, the *cons* of taking the trip. The camera pulls back to show a woman in her office with her walls papered in graphs, charts and spread-sheets, all relating to the possibility of indulging in a Florida Keys vacation. The voice over? "All the *facts* point towards the Florida Keys for your next family vacation." This hits at the very persona of Detail Doris.

Are Your Bagels Hot?

How to Appeal to All of the Senses of Your Customers

The other morning I was sitting in my local bagel shop enjoying my coffee, bagel and newspaper. I am not sure what prompted me to look up, but the first thing that struck me was that this establishment obviously did a booming morning business. People stood in line fifteen deep and didn't seem to mind the wait. As I was pondering the idea of having people stand in line for what *I* have to offer, another curiosity struck me. It had nothing to do with the customers or even the counter personnel. It was the bagel maker who got my attention.

I watched as he carefully manipulated a tray of steaming hot bagels into the metal bins with appropriate labeling according to the flavor. He then proceeded to add a little sign—bright red with white letters—to those bins to which he had just contributed. The sign? "HOT." Nothing extraordinary in and of itself, but the reaction was immediate. The very next patron to order, demanded some of the "hot" bagels. And so did the next. And the next. Soon the bagel maker reappeared with another tray and followed the same routine with another flavor. And guess what? The same results. The customers switched their "flavor-of-the-minute" and their attention to the new bin labeled "HOT."

This little ritual went on for the next forty-five minutes and I felt like I had discovered the marketing idea of the century. I got up the nerve during a lull in the action (there was a few minutes when there were no "hot" bagels available) and I approached the young lady donning the manager nametag. When I inquired as to this phenomenon, she threw back her head and laughed. "You caught us! You uncovered our entire marketing strategy."

My new marketing guru explained to me that the powers-that-be in her company had always subscribed to the idea that to market, one must appeal to as many senses of the customer, or prospective customer, as possible. "Sense of smell and taste were taken care of in this environment," she explained. "But bagels are bagels and they all pretty much look the same." She went on to detail how they had discovered the "HOT" strategy completely by mistake. Originally, they had put the signs on to warn store personnel of the impending danger in handling steaming hot bagels. What they discovered was a huge increase in demand, by their customers, on any particular flavor that was adorned with the little sign. She finished rather defensively by explaining that they did not manipulate their customers, but simply appealed to another sense–sight. I suddenly understood the reason why the shop did not seem to anticipate daily consumption and bake bagels in advance of the rush.

The obvious lesson I took from this is that we must figure out ways to appeal to all of our customer's senses. Some have it easier than others. A restaurateur, a caterer or a florist for example, have a great "one-up" on the banker, the insurance broker or the accountant. The "outside-the-lines" marketing idea that occurred to me was this: How can I entice my customers with the "hot" item or service of the moment? I can't use a little red sign, but I could give the same impression.

One florist, with whom we have consulted, imports Holland tulips during months in which her market typically can't find tulips-hot item! A local restaurateur who promotes a certain type of snapper served a certain kind of way "upon availability" tells me that it is his most popular dish. By the way, I frequent that restaurant and have never been told the snapper is not available—hot item!

The possibilities seem endless. Take a look at your product, your service or even yourself and ask yourself, "Do my customers perceive my 'bagels' as being HOT?"

Does Customer Service Have Anything to Do With Marketing?

Word of Mouth Tells Others About YOU!

GREAT customer service has everything to do with marketing! I tell audiences around the world that customer service is something you offer whether or not you are a company or an individual. It doesn't matter if you are "serving" an internal or an external customer, you have an amazing opportunity to make your mark!

Consider this customer service story. I walked into Nordstrom in the Dallas Galleria intent on purchasing a pair of running shoes I knew they carried. After being approached by a friendly (but not overly-friendly) salesperson named James, he asked me a series of questions about my desire for that particular shoe. By analyzing my answers, James convinced me that another shoe was far more appropriate for the multi-use needs that I had. He went to get me the shoes to try on.

James returned with nothing in his hands and a disappointed look in his eyes. He informed me that he was out of stock but that he could order them and have them delivered to me. Quite honestly, I didn't want the shoes that badly. I am a "instant gratification" kind of guy and if I couldn't have them now, I could find them back home.

James persisted. "Mr. Tobe, are you going to be in the Mall for awhile?" I hesitated but informed him that I planned on having lunch before I left. He replied, "Let me try to find the shoes. Come back when you are finished eating."

I agreed and left thinking that this was odd. There is only one Nordstrom store in Dallas, so how could he produce my shoes in the next forty-five minutes?

When I returned, James was beaming. He had the shoes! As I tried them on I noticed a price tag on the box from an athletic shoe store also found in the mall; a competitor! James had gone to the other store, purchased the shoes and had them ready for me. Not only that, but the price on the tag was two dollars more than the price James was quoting me. When I inquired as to why he had done this, he replied, "Mr. Tobe, it is worth the effort and the extra two dollars to make sure you come back to us next time you are in Dallas"

Needless to say, I had no choice but to buy the shoes right then and there. More importantly, I have now shared this example with hundreds of people in my recent workshops and keynotes. And now I am sharing it with thousands of you!

When you make a great impression, people talk about you. There are all kinds of studies that basically show that if you do something right people will tell many people about their experience. Do something wrong and they will tell many MORE people. We constantly have to keep considering how our actions are going to have repercussions. Like the stone thrown into the smooth waters of the pond—it's all about the ripple!

PSSST→

Look for opportunities to develop a personal and professional friendship. Friends not only will enhance business, but they can bring balance to the pressures of work.

This is just the tip of the iceberg. If you constantly keep word-of-mouth marketing at the top of your mind and if you consistently promote this to your people, you can't help but offer better service and a better buying experience. Someone once said that it is not the problems in business that can kill you—it's what you do OR don't do about them!

Experience Customer Service

It's Gone Beyond Customer Service

Let's talk about customer service! It just has not been discussed, dissected and examined enough over the last few years. (hint of sarcasm there!) In visiting my local bookstore, I realized that there are more books written on customer service than any other business topic today. The sad part is that I also realized that I have read many of them.

Don't get me wrong. There's probably not a more important topic than the "service" we offer our customers, but I think things have changed. Those organizations that recognize the next wave in customer service will be the ones who ultimately "serve" their market better than any others. Those organizations that consider this, will gain the competitive "edge". When you think of organizations the likes of Nordstrom, Saturn, and Starbuck's, we automatically think that customer service is the one thing that separates them from the pack. This is not entirely true.

Imagine for a moment that I have a handful of coffee beans in my palm. I take those beans to my local MacDonald's and they make me a coffee for about eighty cents. Now, take those same beans (alright, maybe you can argue that they are a little better quality bean, but that's inconsequential in this illustration) over to this relatively-new phenomenon called Starbuck's, and they make me a cup of coffee and charge about three dollars. Is the service really any different at Starbuck's vs. MacDonald's? As a matter of fact, the senior citizens at my MacDonald's are the friendliest, most accommodating people I know. No, it's gone beyond customer service.

Continuing on with our handful of coffee beans...

This past February, I had the fortuitous opportunity to spend a few days of R&R on the island of Bali in the South Pacific. Add to that the splendor of the Four Season's Resort—a Five Star hotel—rated in 2004 as one of the top five resorts in the ENTIRE world. Our private,

thatched roof, dining room—open on three sides to the beach and the Pacific—was the setting for breakfast each morning. Remember our coffee beans? A cup of coffee at the Four Season's Hotel cost something in the neighborhood of seven dollars. AND WE PAID IT! Why?

You see, it wasn't the service, although I have NEVER had service as personalized and attentive as we did at this resort. But breakfast, once delivered to our villa, was still just a meal! No, it was THE EXPERIENCE. People are more than willing to pay for the experience if it is unique, personalized and responsive. When was the last time you considered the experience that your client—internal or external—has with you each time they interact with you? From the first moment they make contact with you until the moment they are finished with you. It's no longer about customer service but rather, it's about the experience.

I tell retailers all of the time to walk into their place of business tomorrow and smell. What is the first thing you see? What is the first thing you hear? This all effects the experience their customers have with them. Sometimes we take things for granted because we have been doing what we do for such a long time. Consider the experience!

My Pizza Joint is YOUR Competition!

Knowing Your Market Better Than Anyone Else

I am not a pizza-eater! I think I got pizza'd out in college. Typically, my family will save their pizza cravings for when I am out on the road and I'm not able to complain that I have nothing to eat.

One evening, my wife called me in a frenzy—late from work. She is a mediator by profession and is one of the best "closers" I know. She reasoned, "If you don't want to order a pizza and find something else for you to eat, then you can make dinner for everyone." I asked the only logical question, "Who do I call to order pizza?"

I found the number to Mama Leone's Pizza—apparently my family's favorite—on a magnet on our refrigerator. After two rings, the phone was answered. "Mama Rocks Pizza. Welcome to the Tobe household!" Now, I am very familiar with caller ID, so I wasn't shocked that the young man knew who was calling. What did surprise me, was the fact that he pronounced my name correctly. Most people say "Tobey" on their first attempt, not the correct pronunciation. Good guess? I wasn't sure.

The voice on the other end continued, "Who am I speaking to this evening?" I replied, "This is Jeff Tobe..." He interrupted, "Oh, Mr. Tobe. You've never called before!"

Ok. I am also familiar with databases, but I must admit that I was intrigued. The voice continued, "Will it be the regular tonight?".

To prove how bizarre a thinker I am, I must admit that it immediately dawned on me that I didn't want to give this guy the information. Remember, my family orders pizza while I am away. I want HIM to tell ME what the "regular" is. If it isn't what my family should be ordering, then I want to know who is ordering pizza from my house when I am not there!

"You tell me what you think the *regular* is," I challenged. He didn't hesitate in replying, "1/2 pepperoni...1/2 plain cheese!" He was right.

It was his next question that sent me reeling. "Mr. Tobe, have you fixed the light on your front porch?"

Understand that my wife has been pestering me for over 2 months to change the light bulb in that fixture, but it is up high and I have to get

the ladder... You get the picture! More inter-
esting, however, was that this guy asked the
question. I could only ask him why. He continued,
"The last time we delivered a pizza, your light was
burned out and my driver had trouble reading
your house number.
I don't want your
pizza to arrive to
you cold."

"It will be fixed
by the time you get
here," was all that
I could blurt out!

The point of
this insight into
the Tobe pizza-
ordering-realm?
This pizza—
according to my
family—is not the
best tasting pizza
in town. But, would

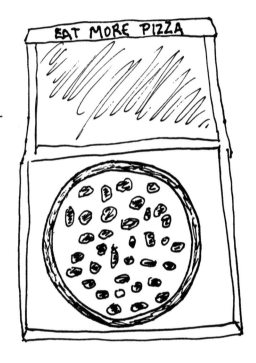

we order from anyone else? I doubt it. You see, it
has nothing to do with the product, but everything to do with the buying experience.

I have considered this the essence of a
successful organization for a long while. It is no
longer "customer service" that sets us apart
from our competition. It is the "customer experi-

ence" that will give us the competitive edge. Think about paradigm-shifting organizations like Saturn, Nordstrom, Cheesecake Factory, and, yes, Mama Leone's Pizza. They do not offer the best product or service. Nor are they just customer service-oriented. They offer a unique customer experience.

Consider the experience your customer has with you. It is the overall impression they have AFTER the transaction is complete. Would they recommend you to others? Do they become what Ken Blanchard calls, "Raving fans", or are they simply satisfied with your customer service? Service, which by the way, is simply *expected* in today's environment. No, things have to go deeper. Beyond service is the emotions I experience during and after our interaction.

My friend at Mama Leone's knew us better than any other pizza joint I could call. He asked the right kinds of questions to ensure that we would call only them the next time we wanted to order pizza. By the way, it turns out that the light fixture on our front porch did not simply need a light bulb, but needed a more complicated 'fix' that I could not provide. So, what did I do? I stood outside with a flashlight and waited for the driver to arrive! Now that's what I call an "experience".

THOUGHTS ON...

Sales

How Well Do You Know Your Customer?

Do You Know Your Customers' Buying Styles?

On a recent cross-country trip, a flight attendant was very attentive to my needs. At one point, she flippantly remarked that I was a "high maintenance" passenger. After I got past my hurt feelings, it occurred to me that maybe she had more insight into her passengers than I had given her credit. When I pressed her for more information, I was surprised to find just how much she could teach me.

She explained that she and her colleagues actually could identify passenger "types" by the way they handed in their cups and other trash, by the demands they made on them and generally by their will-

ingness to chat, sleep or work. She went on to tell me that this was not in their official handbook, but that it came in very handy every single day. Before she left me pondering this unique approach to customer service, she added one more little ditty. She said, "If we get to know them, we can give them what they need before they even ask." What a simple but phenomenally insightful revelation. *Do you know your clients' needs before they even ask?*

If we are to be in complete control of the sales process, we need to first understand our own "selling behavioral style" and second, find a way to quickly identify—and adapt to—any client's "buying behavioral style" as did the flight attendant. Psychologists have agreed for years that there are basically four different "behavior styles" in western society. These styles have been called so many different things by so many studies, tests and instruments, but the fact remains that they all agree on the number four. The one study that I use in all of my sales training was developed by Carlson Learning Systems out of Minneapolis and is referred to as DiSC™. From the matrix below, try to identify your dominant style and keep in mind the following principles:

- We all have each of the 4 tendencies, but we are dominant in one.

- No one style is better than the others.

- We are examining only your "work behavioral style". You have other 'styles' at home, at play, as a parent, etc.

Let's take a look at how to handle each behavioral style in a sales situation.

Dominant

Clients with a high Dominant style—or a High D—are probably the easiest to recognize in a sales situation. They thrive on being in control and will usually ask you to "get to the bottom line". They are seldom concerned with details as long as you can provide what you promise. Because the High D is so task-oriented, you should always talk about the results they will achieve by using your product or service. Always be prepared and look professional with this buyer. As a matter of fact, I suggest that when calling on a new prospect, always treat them like a High D. This way you can't go wrong. I have never encountered a buyer who complained that a salesperson got down to business *too* quickly, but I have met many who rued the days they encountered sales-people who insist on chatting.

By the way, I especially enjoy doing business with a High D. They are less likely to be concerned with price and, of the four styles, are quickest to make a buying decision. They tend to be very loyal clients, until you make one mistake; then they will hunt you down and kill you! Remember, this person needs to be in control, but are concerned with time restraints, so only give them two or three choices. Finally, do not try to use incentives or "specials" or gimmicks with a High D. They just don't get excited about them and, even worse, it makes you less professional in their eyes.

Influence

From my sales training experience, I would venture to guess that the majority of sales-people in the western hemisphere fall under this category. High I's are also very easy to recognize because of their ability to be excellent communicators, friendly and highly social. You will know you are selling to a High I because they will generally want to get to know you a little better. They may suggest meeting over lunch or on the links. Influencers love to generate enthusiasm and, unlike High D's, are very people-oriented rather than task-oriented. If you ask them why they enjoy their work, they will tell you that it has something to do with the people they get to meet and the fun that they have. When you are selling to this style, make sure you emphasize how your solution will make them look great to the people with whom they work. Emphasize the fun they will have or the enjoyment they will get. High I's love "specials" or incentives; especially if it means some type of personal recognition or gain.

The challenge you have in selling to a High I is that you may have trouble keeping their interest when it comes to details. My suggestion is to put all the details in writing after your meeting. High I's are often so disorganized that you can't count on them to remember the facts. When approaching the Influencer, remember to show them testimonials of other recognizable clients who have benefited from your solutions; they love to be in good company. Do not give Influencers a lot of choices as it will just confuse them. Present your *one* best solution with lots of enthusiasm and remember to allow enough time on your sales call for socializing.

Steady

Another very people-oriented style is our Steady buyer or our High S. Unlike our Influencer style, the High S buyer does not like to change too quickly and will take a little more convincing to do so. The High S has traditional values and is motivated by personal stability so we must approach this buyer with a "soft sell". If you are a High D or a High I, you need to calm down and take it slow and easy with your High S client. Your enthusiasm or penchant for wanting to quickly get to the bottom line, will simply turn off this person. The High S style has a knack of taking ideas and putting them into motion, so they are a great person to have on your side. You must provide this person with guarantees of minimum risk. Your solution, including incentives, must be oriented to how it will make the whole department or company look good; remember they are concerned with the "team" effort. Although they may seem slow to change, simply provide them with proof on why a change will be advantageous and, most importantly, show them how your solution will make things run "smoothly". The High S buyer is concerned with how your solution will be implemented so provide details in this area along with a plan on how problems will be corrected. If you want to begin to get on the good side of a High S, simply compliment them on their family; you will find photos all over their office!

Conscientious

The fourth style, is motivated by accuracy in achieving their goals. Recognizing this, successful salespeople orient their solutions to providing details as to why theirs is the "correct" answer to the challenge. You must expect a slower sales cycle with our High C buyers because they need "just one more study" or "one more opinion" before they sign on the dotted line. Like our Dominant style, High C's are very task-oriented and are not interested in socializing. Show them that you have analyzed and prepared your solution. High C's will want to spend time with you going over the details and checking for accuracy. (I recently had a prospect return a proposal so that I could correct the "typos" in the copy!) When selling to a High C, slow down, put all details in writing and don't exaggerate. They are not so concerned with quantity of solutions as with quality. You must be patient and persistent. You will recognize your High C buyer when you receive a phone call from them, eight months after your sales call, and they inform you that they are ready to buy. The problem is that if you are a High D or a High I, you have already erased them from your data bank and written them off as hopeless! Finally, when selling to a High C, establish your credibility by offering both the pros and cons of your solution. If you don't, they will!

> *"If you have anything valuable to contribute to the world, it will come through the expression of your own behavior—that single spark of divinity that sets you off and makes you different from every other living creature."*
> — Bruce Barton

It is only natural that our main interest is what we learn about OUR style. Still, we need to remember that understanding our client's buying

style and being able to adapt to their prefer-
ences, will not only simplify the sales process, but
set us apart as the sales professional. We can
see that each behavioral style has definite
strengths and admirable qualities. Before you can
collaborate effectively and productively with
your clients—before you can establish any kind of
relationship with them—they need to know that
you recognize these qualities in them. By showing
your client that, in spite of your differences, you
understand, appreciate and even value their individual behavioral strengths, you build a ground
work of mutual trust and respect. Then, and only
then, may you anticipate their needs before they
express them.

Salesperson Appreciation Day

How Creativity and Sales Go Hand-in-Hand

I would like to suggest that we lobby whomever needs to be lobbied in Washington to establish an official Salesperson Appreciation Day! For one day each year, our clients would have to bow to *our* needs, jump when we say jump, and follow us around for one day telling us just how creative we really are in this industry. Only one piece of advice, "don't hold your breath while we are trying to get this done!"

Short of a special day, I think it is important for all salespeople to stand back and give themselves a standing ovation once and awhile. In speaking to thousands of people every year, I have come to understand just how little innovative and creative thinking salespeople are appreciated in our "do-more-with-less" world.

Creativity in sales is the least appreciated, least understood of all our skills.

And, in times of volatility and change, our most needed one.

Often, we fail to understand our own creativity because of the labels normally applied to the term. In one recent study, more than 130 buyers were asked to describe creative salespeople.

They're "zany" or "artists," they said. They're "off the wall." "Creative salespeople are hard to manage, difficult to nail down; they like to make their own rules."

Creativity, at least in terms of sales importance, can be much more clearly defined. I believe that creativity and resourcefulness are much the same thing. Resourcefulness is the trait we must develop in ourselves if we want control over the sales situation. If we examine the word resourcefulness, we see that it is little more than creativity: The ability to bring something into existence that does not yet exist, the skill of dealing with any kind of sales challenge.

Harry Pickens, a professor at University of Florida, put it best in a recent keynote address I attended, when he talked about seeing the "invisible". Our ability in any profession to see opportunities where others see limitations, is what defines success. If we don't appreciate our creativity, our clients certainly can't be expected to.

While sitting in the lobby of a hotel in Orlando, I struck up a conversation with a woman who proudly explained that she was an event planner. She explained that she was new to the profession and new to sales. Her background was actually in accounting. She was middle-aged, lived in a small mid-western town with her husband and two kids. She was about as far from "zany" as you can get.

But, when she spoke about her new career, her creative resourcefulness came through loud and clear. Bobbi had lost her job several months before and soon after, decided to work closer to home. "I was tired of commuting," she explained. "It's worth a drop in salary not to have to go into that city every day."

With her husband, Bobbi spent a weekend driving around some of the new commercial areas within a certain radius of their home, noting the names of larger companies. She began applying to these firms. One, in particular, captured her fancy—a growing special events company.

At first, Bobbi approached the company in a traditional way. She sent a resume and followed up with a phone call. To the company's credit, they had decided that they were no longer going to hire "anyone who breaths and can sell", and they politely explained that they had no need for a numbers person in the firm at that time.

Not to be discouraged, she took a different tack. Checking business directories, Bobbi found the name of the owner of the company. Rather than just make your traditional cold call, Bobbi started asking everybody she knew whether or not they had done business with this person. She found out that her baby-sitter's mother was a copier salesperson and had just sold the firm a new copier. Bobbi spoke to the woman, trying to gain some insight into the owner's mindset. She found out that the owner was very progressive and valued "creativity".

Bobbi called the owner directly and simply explained how 'creative' she had been in getting to him; resourcefulness at its best. The owner agreed to meet with her and hired her on the spot. I can only guess that he recognized the opportunity to hire someone, no matter their background, who had the drive and *resourcefulness* to get what they wanted.

I asked Bobbi, "Have you always been creative like this?"

"Creative?" Bobbi replied, puzzled. "I think of it more as determined." She chuckled. "I'm certainly not creative."

UGH! This is what tears at my very being. *If we can't appreciate our own creativity, innovation and resourcefulness, how can we expect our clients to?*

What you must realize is that dogged determination is necessary to overcome obstacles that normally stop other people. There is a true creative force in salespeople like Bobbi. Their willingness to see beyond the obstacles allows them to use their imagination to conjure up solutions that have never existed before.

Every day should be our own "Salesperson Appreciation Day". Why wait for our clients to declare it? It may never happen. It has to start with you.

Frequent Flier Pointers

Four Lessons We Need to Know About Our Clients

If, like myself, you are a "road warrior" and you play the frequent flier game, you can appreciate how frustrating it is to have to travel on one of those *other* airlines. You know! The one where you have no status. Where you are treated like a plebian and you look for horror stories to relate to your friends. A few weeks ago, I looked forward to the unpleasant duty of having to fly on one these inferior lines in order to make a connection to another city.

Now, I also must share with you that, if given the choice, I prefer to travel cross-country in very comfortable clothing. It is not unusual to find me in warm up pants, a golf shirt and sneakers. On the day of this 'flight into the unknown", I arrived at the airport dressed in this fashion.

I finally made it to a ticket agent, after having to wait in the "commoner's line", and was greeted by an abnormally large smile on a woman in about

her late 50's. The first words out of her mouth?
"Guess you're not used to having to wait in line?"
I was skeptical as to why she said that. I
certainly didn't look the part of a person not
used to being kept waiting. She noticed my inquis-
itive look and she drew my attention to the
luggage tag on my briefcase now sitting on the
counter in front of her. It indicates that I am the
top 'tier' of my preferred airline. "What can we
do to make you change that tag to one of ours
by the end of this year?"

Lesson number one—Do any of us take the time
to look for indications that our customers or
prospects are already loyal to one of our competitors? Do we then take this information and
process it to our advantage? This woman had a
choice. She could have dismissed me as one of
"their" customers or she could take this one
opportunity–without having a second chance as
far as she knew–to convert me to their product
or service.

I found it difficult to answer her question
concerning how they could win my loyalty. I was
very fond of my airline. And I know the hassles
and tribulations one must go through to begin a
new frequent flier program anew. I looked at her
and sheepishly shrugged my shoulders.

Lesson number two—Do you understand the
huge discrepancy between what your prospect
perceives as the *cost* of doing business with you

versus the *value* of doing business with you?
Remember, this is not reality—this is *their* perception. We must see the world through our clients'
eyes to see the way our client buys.

Almost as if she had read my mind, the woman
allayed my fears. "I can imagine how the thought
of starting all over with a new airline must para-
lyze a lot of frequent travelers like you. I would
like you to give us a fair try. Would it help if I
offered you an upgrade to first class on this
cross-country trip?"

Now, as many of you are self-employed
professionals are aware, First Class is a self-
indulgence afforded to us by our airline because
of our status, but not for which we would
consider paying on *any* carrier. I turned to my
new friend and graciously accepted her offer
while biting my tongue in glee. She floored me with
her next request. "Unfortunately, we have a dress
code in our First Class cabin," she explained. She
proceeded to walk out from behind the counter
and survey me from head to foot. With an
unapologetic look she continued, "If you would
be willing to change into something a little more
professional, I would be glad to upgrade you."

What's one to do? Compromise one's very
comfort? Acquiesce to such an obviously insane
dress policy? *Absolutely!* I asked where the
nearest men's room was located and told her to

hang on to her upgrade. Within three minutes I was back, having fulfilled my part and waiting to consummate the deal. True to her word, she handed me a shiny new folder—the one that proudly displays the words FIRST CLASS on the outside—and I proudly proceeded to my gate.

Lesson number three—ASK! How many opportunities have we missed because we did not ask? If our prospects or clients want something from us that badly, we can basically ask them to do what it takes to get it. Once we understand who it is with whom we are dealing, it puts us in the preverbal driver's seat.

Last week I was flying on my original airline once again (it takes time for the "weaning" process!). I struck up a conversation with my seatmate—in first class of course! With his baby finger extended as he sipped his tea, he explained to me that he too "endured" that other airline just the week before and was abhorred by their lack of customer service. Before I could defend my new friends, he finished with, "They do tell a good story however. The woman at the ticket counter told me that she once actually got some guy to change his clothes just to get an upgrade. Can you imagine being that desperate to fly first class?"

Lesson number four—It's all in your perspective. I sat there thinking to myself that this guy didn't even know the half of it! Had the ticket agent asked me to be loyal to them for the next three months *and* stand on my head, I probably would have done that as well.

Motivation Is Us!

Five Truths That Prevent You From Motivating Others

In these downsized times, the number one question I get asked by sales managers in any industry is, "How do we motivate our people or our buyers and keep them motivated to sell/buy more?" I have thought a lot about motivation because it is not uncommon for someone to introduce me as a *motivational* speaker. Something about that appellation has bothered me since I first got into professional speaking and something about being asked how to motivate salespeople has also been a tough quandary. Then it struck me one day during a three-day sales training session with a large promotional products distributor...

You can't motivate your people to sell for you, any more than you can motivate your clients to buy from you!

1. You cannot motivate other people!

Motivation is a fire from within. If someone else tries to light that fire under you, chances are it will burn very briefly.

— Stephen Covey

What we have to realize is that we can give people incentives to perform better and encourage and support their efforts, but the basic motivation for their behavior must come from within. People motivate themselves. All we can do as a manager or as a salesperson, is create an environment that aids in motivating someone to do something. For example, I recently spoke to one of the top salespeople at a large corporation in Pittsburgh. She explained to me that her sales manager was a wonderful man who kept her motivated at all times. Knowing what I have discovered, I probed deeper and found that, in fact, the sales manager just understood his salespeople's individual likes and dislikes and structured an environment around those things that turned on his people. Posters around the office, an open door policy and a bi-annual customer focus group, added to creating that environment that is essential for salespeople to motivate themselves. How can you create the environment to motivate yourself?

2. All people are motivated!

I can't imagine a person becoming a success who doesn't give this game of life everything he's got.

– Walter Cronkite

This is probably the most controversial thing I share with both salespeople and sales managers. Most of you probably know someone that you feel just isn't motivated at all. Maybe it's one of your clients with whom you just can't find the right "button" to push. Maybe it's a co-worker with whom you have tried dangling the proverbial "carrot" with no response. Actually, research indicates that *all people are motivated*, no matter how they're behaving! Say, for example, Joan is working at a slow pace. Her manager may assume Joan is lazy or "unmotivated". But she actually may be motivated by a desire to achieve perfection. If the task requires speed instead of perfection, Joan's manager needs to coach her to help her adapt her behaviors, but there is no need to motivate her. Even when someone is inactive, they are still motivated. In this case, they are motivated to do nothing!

3. People do things for their reasons, not yours!

Getting down to the nitty-gritty, most people are motivated by unconscious motives most of the time.

– Richard J. Mayer

Although this may seem selfish, we have to realize that self-interest is simply a question of survival for many salespeople and clients. Even if we can't directly motivate others, we can better relate with people if we approach them with the desire to find out their reasons for doing what they do—or not doing what you would like them to do. In this new "relationship selling" world in which we operate, putting yourself in the client's shoes will better help you understand their reasons for behaving the way they do. There is a saying that I share in all of my training; "See the world through your client's eyes and you'll see the way your client buys!"

4. Too much of one motivation can become a limitation!

Awareness of both your limitations and your potential enhances humility.
— Sheila Murray Bethel

Tom, a computer programmer who attended one of my creativity workshops, related to me that he had recently received a promotion to division head. His analytical programming skills were highly touted throughout his international firm. In his new position, Tom applied the same painstaking care and delibera- tion to minor administrative

issues as he did to his programming projects, and as a result, he was perceived as slow and often indecisive. Because of his tendency to research everything, some workers felt he didn't trust their judgment. His strength had definitely become a limitation. When dealing with certain clients, our strengths as salespeople–ie. the gift of gab, the ability to chatter excessively–may just become our limitations even though that is what motivates us on a daily basis. Our role, in this new selling environment, is to identify the buying style of our client and adapt to that. Fellow sales trainer and journalist, Jeffrey Gitomer says, "People don't like to be sold but they love to buy!" I tell salespeople all of the time to stop selling! Figure out how I buy and present your ideas, your service or your product to me in a way in which I will buy into it! Not in a way in which you are used to selling it.

5. If I know more about you than I have before, I can manage the sale

The business of expanding your consciousness is not an option. Either you are expandable or you are expendable.

— Robert Schuller

This goes against the old salesperson's credo, "Thou shalt not out talk the salesperson". As I share in my book, *The Sales Coach*, we need to ask more questions of those who work for us and of those who buy from us. We have to establish (and for many it's a case of re-establishing) our role as the seeker of information and the client's role as giver. Once we truly understand the power of controlling communication in creating a motivational environment, we can understand how we can also influence the entire sales process.

Many of us think we know ourselves pretty well, and yet we still are surprised by the way people react at times to the things we do or say. Our challenge is to recognize both our strengths and limitations so that we remain in control of our own motivation, particularly in those situations where we find ourselves typically uncomfortable or ineffective. We all know that we cannot change someone's behavior unless they are willing to change it themselves. When it comes to the sales process, we cannot change a client's motivation to buy, but we can simply provide them with an environment that makes it easier to do business with us over our competitors.

Is motivation permanent? I think Zig Ziglar, the guru of inspiration, answers that best:

"Of course motivation isn't permanent. But then, neither is bathing; but it is something you should do on a regular basis."

It's Kind of Hard to Explain

People Do Business With People Who Seem to Love What They Do for a Living

Do you find it difficult to explain just what it is you do for a living sometimes? This has been a perplexing dilemma for me over the past 9 years until I traveled with my wife to Dallas earlier this year. I THINK I HAVE THE ANSWER, but first, let me fill you in on the earth-shattering experience that revealed this answer to me.

My wife and I were joined by friends of ours for dinner at a new restaurant in Dallas. These friends simply explained that they had been told that this new establishment had received rave reviews from everyone who had eaten there; they knew nothing else about it. The name of the restaurant? "ENIGMA".

Now, I pride myself on having a fairly extensive vocabulary, but the meaning of this word escaped me. I decided to check it out in a dictionary. The best explanation I could find?

"Something that is difficult or hard to explain."

What an odd name for a restaurant!

Before we were even seated, I knew that Enigma was going to be an eating experience we weren't soon to forget. With only about ten tables, I understood why our friends had had to make reservations over one month prior to our arrival. My first observation was the outrageous decorations, including ten tables that were completely different in design with no chairs that matched each other.

Our table was set with completely different dishes and silverware. I don't mean that each setting was different but that even at one place-setting none of the plates, none of the silver patterns, nor none of the glasses matched each other.

We ordered some "adult beverages" and when they were delivered to our table we were amused at the fact that, although two of us had asked for the same drink, one glass was a regular eight-ounce water glass and the next was no smaller than a birdbath! Our server explained that it was simply "luck of the draw" as to which glass you received.

Next, our waitress handed each of us three different, very creative menus. Each of us had three different menus—12 menus total. We had to trade menus amongst the four of us to get an overall concept of the fare.

Besides the odd selections available on the menu, our waitress also explained that even if two of us ordered the same selection, she could not guarantee that they would come out prepared the same way. She could not even inform us of the side dishes that came with each selection. "This is why we are an enigma," she explained. "You have to give our chefs total creative freedom to prepare your meal."

She was absolutely correct. My wife's Mahi-Mahi came soaked in a wonderful green tamale sauce while my female friend's Mahi-Mahi came wrapped in a beautiful tureen with a white vegetable sauce. The rest of the meal was...it was...nothing short of an enigma!

Always in search of a great analogy to share with my audiences, by dessert I had had a mild epiphany! I knew the exact answer everyone is supposed to give when queried about what it is we do for a living. What I do is an *enigma.*

That's all you need to say to get someone's attention. When it comes to the creativity that you offer, the service or product you can customize and the challenges you can solve, it *should* be hard to explain. That's the lure!

The mystery surrounding this new explanation of your profession, may just be the thing that will attract customers, making *you* so popular that your planner will be full. Every time they call you to ease a pain, they should have no idea what you are going to serve. They should however, sit back, enjoy the experience and trust that you will be creative each and every time they *experience* your expertise.

You see, it occurred to me that our job is not just to solve a business challenge but, like my dining adventure in Dallas, we must give our clients an EXPERIENCE every single time they require our expertise. Never give them the same menu when they ask you to wait on them. Never serve their solutions on the same plate or in the same glass.

Why fight it? What you do is probably an *enigma* and you should all be proud to demonstrate the mystery every time your client calls.

By the way, we paid more for our meal at Enigma than I have ever spent on dinner in my life! Do I care? Absolutely not. It was worth the experience. Is your client willing to pay for the "experience" they have with you?

Listen to Your World...

Effective Listening Techniques to Make You a Better Salesperson

I want to share with you the number one, outside-the-lines, only-found-here, sure- to-make-you-a-million, sales technique that until now has remained a mystery to most salespeople. Those rare people who have discovered this one "tool", have gone on to change the world as we know it.

Now, it is going to require most of you to get outside of your comfort zone to be willing to try something that does not come naturally for most business professionals. When we concentrated on this in our business, it increased our sales by 37 percentage in one year. What is it you ask? It's our ability to listen!

Now, don't guffaw and roll your eyes. I have proven that listening, as an effective sales tool, can increase a salesperson's bottom line by up to 40 percent.

You may not have realized that listening is such an important, yet often overlooked, business skill. We spend 70 percentage of our waking hours in verbal communication. Listening, as a method of taking in information, is used far more than reading and writing combined. Isn't your job—no matter the industry—to listen, to process what we hear and then to react?

An informal definition of listening, is simply, taking in information from our consumers while remaining nonjudgmental and empathetic. It involves acknowledging the consumer in a way that invites the communication to continue by providing limited, but encouraging input carrying an idea one step forward.

The challenge we have is that when we think about listening, we tend to assume it is basically the same as hearing. This is a dangerous assumption because it leads us to believe effective listening is instinctive. As a result, we make little effort to learn or develop listening skills and unknowingly neglect a vital function of communication that results in miscommunication and ultimately loss of market share. To paraphrase Dr. Stephen Covey author of *7 Habits of Highly*

Effective People, "One of the basic of all human needs is to understand and to be understood." Our clients need to know that we understand their concerns and needs.

Let's look at seven techniques to becoming a better listener. Although these focus on the literal aspects of the personal listening process, I have prompted you to think about how they apply to your marketing and sales challenges as well.

1. Listen with your Eyes and your Ears

Many times someone's body is telling much more than their words. Many studies have been conducted in this area and most concur that the words that we use in communicating with each other, account for less than 10 percent of our total message. The tone of our voice accounts for somewhere around 30 percent and our body language makes up about 60 percent of our message. ARE YOU ACTUALLY WATCHING FOR YOUR CUSTOMER'S REACTIONS TO YOUR COMPANY'S "BODY LANGUAGE" OR ARE YOU SIMPLY LISTENING TO THEIR WORDS?

2. Never Interrupt

Interrupting another person does not necessarily involve speaking up at an inappropriate time. We interrupt others when we argue mentally with something that is said, when we disagree with a point that is made or when we allow our minds to wander. Even if the purpose of your communication is to present information or describe your services, try to do less than 50% of the talking. Most of what you say should be in the form of questions to prompt the client to give you more information—not to be seen as an interruption. Once the other person perceives you to be competing with them to speak, they may become too uncomfortable to give you the real message. As a rule of thumb, before speaking, pause and count to five after the other person stops talking. ARE YOU ASKING YOUR CUSTOMERS FOR THEIR FEEDBACK WITHOUT INTERRUPTING?

3. Ignore Distractions

We are perceived as being an empathetic listener when we learn to ignore distractions of any kind. We have to visually mentally and emotionally focus on the speaker. Listen with your eyes, ears and heart. Tell yourself, "I'll listen to this person only." DO YOUR CLIENTS TRULY BELIEVE YOU ARE LISTENING TO JUST THEM—ONE AT A TIME—OR DO THEY FEEL THAT YOU ARE TOO DISTRACTED BY OTHER CONCERNS?

4. Model Positive Behavior

Your modeling during conversations can set a positive atmosphere that encourages trust and inspires the client to open up to you. We must model behavior that we have observed from those whom we consider to be excellent listeners and role models. DOES YOUR COMPANY MODEL OTHER COMPANIES WHO YOUR CONSUMERS BELIEVE LISTEN TO THEIR NEEDS?

5. Restatement and Feelings Check

Our goal in becoming an empathetic listener is to listen for content and feeling, understanding the message on all levels. If your intuition tells you that the other person really means something other than what he is saying, check it out. Restate what you believe is the message and combine it with a "feelings" word to prove or disprove your assumption. For example, when I hear someone say, "I didn't get the service I expected when I called your company," I might reply, "It sounds like you were really disappointed with your last experience." Not only did I restate in other words, what I thought I heard, but I added the word *disappointed.* Now the customer can agree or correct you allowing us to keep on track. WHEN WAS THE LAST TIME YOU CLARIFIED WHAT YOU THINK YOUR CUSTOMERS ARE SAYING?

6. Ambiguity is Reality

The 500 most commonly used words in English have 14,070 dictionary meanings. It is important that you concentrate on the connotation—what words mean through implication and suggestion-vs. denotation or the specific dictionary meaning. DOES YOUR MARKET REALLY UNDERSTAND WHAT YOU ARE ATTEMPTING TO ACCOMPLISH?

7. Ask Questions

It seems like such an easy thing to do, but it is probably the most difficult. We are not natural questioners. We naturally want to be the "giver of information" not the "seeker". Change your role and observe the results you get. ARE YOU ASKING ENOUGH PROBING QUESTIONS OF YOUR CUSTOMERS?

The bottom line is that we can only increase our sales presence by truly listening to our clients. There is a saying I share with all of my training audiences. *Listen to your environment for whispers of opportunity.* Are you really listening for the opportunity in your market?

That is The Question

Digging Deeper to Understand Your Clients' True Needs

I recall an incident several years ago, when I had just started my business and one of my salespeople, Vic, came to me with exciting news. During their first week "knocking on doors", they had secured a $10,000 order. Now, keep in mind that this was back in 1983 and an order of this magnitude was not a common occurrence.

When I interrogated Vic, I discovered that he only had sketchy details. The client had purchased three thousand imprinted coffee mugs because of a 'supplier special'. I asked Vic, "What are they doing with the mugs?"

He hesitated before answering, "Well, they are going to give them away."

"Who are they giving them to?" I wanted to know.

"I have no idea, but I got the purchase order," Vic answered defensively.

As I pondered this new role, I realized that the transformation from selling stuff to selling solutions, lie in the questions we asked of our clients. As odd as it may seem, I decided that there was a huge difference between a large sale and a small sale. Before you dismiss me as a crackpot let me explain. It occurred to me, at that moment, that this was a very typical sale in most industries. As long as we get the sale, who cares how the client is using our service or product?

Typically and traditionally, we have defined the size of the sale in terms of dollar amount. What if I told you that I decided that Vic's ten-thousand-dollar sale was actually a "small" sale? I think we should begin defining the "large" sale as *that which advances us towards building an on-going relationship with our client.* In other words, the more we position ourselves as a "counselor" in our business, the more likely we are to develop that long-term relationship that so many of us seek. I guarantee that Vic had to go in and "sell" that coffee mug client every time he visited them. And, selling the client means that you are not taking the time to properly consult with the client.

In our new role as counselor, I would encourage you to develop a questionnaire that just includes simple questions that must be answered in order for us to be effective for our client. Although your questions may vary from mine, I found these very helpful.

• What are your goals?

Such a simple question can set us apart as the professionals in our area of expertise. When the client insists that they want one hundred widgets, it is our duty to ask, "Why" or "What do you hope to accomplish with these widgets?" You would be amazed at how many clients have not considered this. They get it in their heads that they want sweaters when, in fact, they are going to the equator on their sales trip and golf shirts just may be better received.

• Who is the target audience?

There are many times that I find the buyer is purchasing an item or service that they want, not what their recipient wants. Why not sit with the buyer and put together a "recipient profile", a list of characteristics of the end user. You just might surprise the buyer by making them realize that they need to pay more attention to the demographics of their audience not their partic-ular likes and dislikes.

- # Who makes the buying decision?

So many salespeople forget to ask this going into the sale, that it sometimes throws the buyer off. One rule in our office...if this person can't say YES, then who can? If this person is the person charged with the task of "screening" vendors, then rehearse them to take the details to the decision maker. Just make sure you know how the decision is made and by whom.

- # What is the time schedule?

If you have ever participated in any type of goal-setting course, you were most likely told that goals must be benchmarked against the acronym, SMART. Every goal must be Specific, Measurable, Attainable, Realistic and Timed. This question just zeros in on the "T"—timed. Then make sure it fits all of the others and, most important, is the timing realistic?

- # What is the budget and how is it broken down?

I have ulterior motives for asking this question. I want to know if my sale was part of a larger program or if it was a stand-alone expenditure. This often helps me in securing an even larger sale because the client might not realize that there are other products or services that I can offer as they relate to this project. Not only that, but I need to have a workable—and realistic —budget with which to work. I can't tell you how many times a client suggested a "range" of a budget. This doesn't help me in my quest to adhere to SMART; it is not specific.

- ## What did you like and dislike about the vendor who supplied you with this product/service last time?

A simple question, but an important one if you are to provide service above and beyond what this person expects. If you supplied the product last time, ask it about yourself... you might be surprised by the response.

- ## Is this project going out for bid?

My favorite question. Be careful if you choose to ask this. The client will typically come back with, "Why do you want to know?" Now, I do not promote projecting an image of your company that you cannot support, but on the other hand, sometimes you can get around the issue and get your point across. My reply was always the same..."If this is going out to bid, I will be happy to give it to my bid department. If it is *not* going out to bid, I will give it to my creative department!" Inevitably, the reaction was the same. Nobody wants to sacrifice creativity when it comes to their project. More importantly, I refused to spend the same amount of time on a project that was going out for bid.

These are only suggested questions. The important part is that you simply ask more questions. Our roles have changed from the "giver of information" to that of "the seeker of information" and the only way that we can do this, is to ask more questions of our clients.

By the way, I am sure you are wondering...we did not refuse the ten-thousand-dollar order for coffee mugs nor did we call the client on the phone and ask "Why did you order these?" Hey, we decided to be counselors *after* that sale!

COLORING...

The Poem

Coloring Outside The Lines

Coloring outside the lines is scary business.

Some days, I don't have the courage for it at all.

On my big, bold days though, I like to let my red crayon

just streak across the lines

out there with my purple

in perfect freedom—NO LINES!

And coloring outside the lines is lonely too.

I'm the only kid that doesn't get a gold star on my paper.

The teacher frowns. The kids?

They call me weird or dumb or stupid.

Why don't they see?

I'm not behind them. I'm actually out in front—
running free—
 outside the lines.

And, it would be nice to have a friend who
 colored outside the lines too.

Would you?

— Anonymous

Give the Gift of
Coloring Outside the Lines™
to Your Friends and Colleagues

CHECK YOUR LEADING BOOKSTORE OR ORDER HERE

❏YES, I want _____copies of *Coloring Outside the Lines*™ at $19.95 each, plus $3 shipping per book (Pennsylvania residents please add $1.20 sales tax per book). Orders for 24 or more books, please call for volume discounts. Canadian orders must be accompanied by a postal money order or check in U.S. funds. Allow 15 days for delivery.

❏YES, I am interested in having Jeff Tobe speak or give a seminar to my company, association, or organization. Please send information.

My check or money order for $_____ is enclosed.

Please charge my: ❏Visa ❏Mastercard ❏Discover ❏American Express

Name _____

Organization _____

Address _____

City/State/Zip _____

Phone _____ E-mail _____

Card # _____

Exp. Date _____ Signature _____

Please make your check payable and return to:

Coloring Outside the Lines
200 James Place, Suite 400 • Monroeville, PA 15146

Call your credit card order to: 800-875-7106
Fax: 412-373-8773